Bringing Home the

BAKING

How to Start a Licensed
Home-Based Baking Business

Quincella C. Geiger

Cover photo by Eric Johnson

Printed in the United States of America

ISBN 13: 978-0-615-14518-1

This book is dedicated to my Grandmother Hattie,
who gave me my first baking experiences.
Without her love, support, guidance, and strict discipline,
I would not have taken the path that led me
to opening a baking business and writing this book.

I LOVE YOU, MAMA!

YOUR PARTICIPATION IS WELCOME!

The author and editor have made every effort to make this guide informative, accurate and user- friendly. However, many things can change after publication; businesses close, addresses and phone numbers change, ownership changes, etc.

I would love to hear from you concerning your experiences with this guide.

Please send your comments and suggestions to:

Unique Occasions
P.O. Box 491090
Atlanta, GA 30349

Or e-mail me at: OccasionsUnique@aol.com

Thanks for your purchase and input!

CONTENTS

Acknowledgments

A very special thanks to my sister Janet.
You're the wind beneath my wings.

To Brent, thanks for all of the great advice
and your undying support.

To my dad and all of my wonderful family and great friends,
thanks for your love and support and for always being there for me.

INTRODUCTION

I've been asked many times throughout the years: How did you get your business started from home? How did you get a business license? Where did you find equipment? Where do you purchase supplies? Where do you get great recipes? How do you find customers? I've answered these questions and many more in personal conversations, through e-mails, by phone, and by giving away many of my resource booklets and catalogs.

After years of assisting and encouraging others, I decided to put my experiences, knowledge, and research into this book. While there have been many books over the years dedicated to the start-up and operation of food businesses like restaurants, coffee shops, dessert shops, and storefront bakeries, to my knowledge there is very little detailed information in book or pamphlet form on a home-based baking business. I'm speaking of a step-by-step guide that starts with the basics (careful planning before any money is spent) and takes you through the entire start-up process to the point that your bakery is set up, approved by the health/agriculture department, and fully operational. This is that book.

However, I wanted to provide you with more than how to get a great start with your business, so I didn't stop there. I've also shared my experiences and knowledge of purchasing supplies, creating the best products, finding great recipes (if you don't already have them), marketing, advertising, maintaining your hard-earned accounts, providing great customer service, and much,

much more.

There is one chapter ("Where to Find It") that I feel deserves a special mention—not because it's more important than the other chapters, but because it was a big part of my initial thoughts and reasons for writing this book. When I started my business, I spent many precious hours and days searching for specialty ingredients, packaging supplies, baking pans at wholesale prices, user-friendly tools, and more. If this "Where to Find It" chapter or similar information had been available to me, it would have saved me lots of time, money, and frustration. In consideration of the long hours and work ahead of you, I decided to include my best sources (companies) for everything to start up and operate your business, along with all of their contact information. All you'll need is a phone or access to the Internet and you're ready to go.

Starting a home-based baking business is one of the smartest and most cost-effective ways to try out your products in the marketplace, build your business skills, and get a good feel for what's required if you decide to open a business outside of your home. A little research will reveal that many successful people started their baking businesses from home. If you listen to their stories carefully, you will find, in most cases that their successes didn't come easily and didn't happen overnight. For most people, it was a long process and required many sacrifices.

My intent in writing this book was to draw on my years in the business to make things a little easier, less time-consuming, and more profitable for you. Whether you're interested in a part-time or full-time home-based baking business, this book is for you! The food business, particularly sweets, can be fun, exciting, gratifying, fulfilling, and very profitable. If this is your passion, go for it!

HAPPY BAKING AND MUCH SUCCESS!

—Q. C. G.

Chapter 1

Expectations

What should you expect from your home-based baking business?

RISK

Comparatively speaking, the risk is little to none, and the start-up cost is minimal. Making changes such as electrical wiring, plumbing, painting, and floor covering to a room or area in your home should increase the value of your property. That's a gain, not a loss. If later you decide that you're not happy with the business and you want out, any equipment that you purchased can be sold with an ad through your local newspaper. I've sold equipment and baking pans this way. It works. Be assured, this is not a high-risk business.

DEMANDS

As with many other things in life, you get out what you put in. The rewards from this business will be a result of how much time and resources you're willing to invest. Here are a few critical and necessary ingredients. Some of these will come to mind immediately when you think of starting and operating any business. Some you might not consider until you're faced with a problem.

- A Plan for Your Business

  The mention of writing a business plan scares most people because it's usually lengthy, it asks many questions for which you have no immediate answers, it requires research, and it pushes you to think about things that seem boring, unnecessary, and unrelated to operating *your* business. While a formal business plan (similar to the one outlined by the Small Business Administration) might not be necessary for the start-up of your home-based business, it is necessary and critical that you have a plan. Your plan can be a simple, written road map starting with where you are, where you want to go, and the details of what and how much it will take to get there.

  If your goal is to operate the business full time, you'll need to take a serious, realistic look at everything that's involved before you start to spend money. A business plan outline from the SBA can be found on their Web site at www.sba.gov. If the business plan is intended for your use only and you are not seeking investment funds or a loan from a financial institution (like a bank), the business plan outline at the end of chapter 3 will work well for you.

- Self-Motivation

  When the alarm goes off, *your* drive and enthusiasm must get you out of bed to get the day started. If orders are promised on a certain day and time, you won't have a boss or supervisor to compel you to start preparing in time so that the orders are ready on time. If business is slow and you need to make sales calls or hand out product samples, you won't have anyone to push or force you to do this. If you have problems getting up, getting out, and being productive, your business may never start. If it does, you will definitely have problems with sales and growth. At the beginning of each day, remind yourself of this: no work, no reward.

- Hard Work

  Being the owner/operator of any new business can be difficult. Now add to that the labor involved in a baking business. I know from experience that it's easy, fun, and exciting to answer the phone and take orders for products or download orders from a Web site. That feeling and mood can change when the time comes to turn those work orders into finished products. A home-based baking business will test your motivation, dedication, and endurance. It's a "roll up your sleeves" and "get busy" kind of business. Just remember, great ideas and good intentions alone won't make the business work.

- Lots of Time and Long Hours

    If your goal is growth for the business or taking it from part-time to full-time, be prepared to work lots of early mornings, late nights, and some weekends. Project and order deadlines will often force you to put other things aside, such as a planned getaway, social events, and time with family and friends.

- Responsibility

    If you're a sole proprietor, the responsibility for everything falls on you. If your help doesn't show for work, you're responsible for doing their part and yours. If something breaks, malfunctions, or doesn't happen on schedule, you're responsible for repairs, rescheduling, and possibly an apology to your customer. Until your business has grown and developed to the point that you can hire *responsible* employees, *you wear all the hats*.

- Money Management

    The following are three aspects of money management that will be important in the start-up and operation of your home-based business.

    Shrewd buying. This means taking the time to research (from more than one source) every item or service used in your business. Compare prices (including cost of shipping), compare quality, and then make the best all-around purchase decisions. These decisions will have a huge impact on your profit or loss in the business.

    Accurate bookkeeping. This requires saving receipts from all of your business transactions, no matter how small. These receipts or transactions should be logged into a computerized bookkeeping system or entered into a ledger by hand the old-fashioned way. Your tax preparer can give you tips on the best and most user-friendly computer software. Why should you be so concerned about accurate records? Accurate records can give you quick month-to-month and year-to-year comparisons of how your business is progressing or not progressing. Accurate records are necessary if you want to take advantage of the many tax deductions allowed by the IRS. If you decide to bring in a partner or if you have the need for additional funds to operate or expand the business, you will definitely need accurate records to show your financial position.

Cash flow. Simply put, cash flow is having enough money at all times to purchase products, advertise, do marketing, pay bills, and cover emergencies and any other business expenses. This means that you cannot spend everything you make. A certain amount of money must be held or reinvested to keep the business going. Here's a scenario that illustrates the need for cash flow: Let's say you've done well enough to develop a few wholesale accounts, and you also have a couple of retail corporate accounts. Let's also say that these companies will only pay from invoices on net fifteen or net thirty terms. This means you will receive payment fifteen to thirty days after the invoices are submitted. If processing these orders cleans out your account or available funds, how will you continue to operate and fill orders for the next few weeks? This is when adequate cash flow becomes critical. By the way, experience has taught me that invoices are very often not paid in fifteen or thirty days as promised. If you think that adequate cash flow is unnecessary for a home-based business, you're very wrong. During my years in business, I've experienced the pain of lacking funds to restock supplies, advertise (when it was desperately needed), and sometimes pay bills. Don't let this happen to you. Always put aside a portion of your sales and income for cash-flow needs.

- Professionalism

  This is your business, not a hobby, and you must handle it as such. You must dress appropriately on sales or marketing appointments, particularly if your aim is to do business with businesses. Your product must be appropriately packaged. Your marketing information (business cards, etc.) must be professional. Your customer service should always be professional. Working from home is just as serious a business as working from a retail store. Always project the right image.

- Passion

  Love and passion for what you do will keep you going when things get difficult or seem impossible.

- Patience, Patience, and More Patience

  Things won't always happen on your schedule. Potential customers won't always call back with a response to your marketing and samples as quickly as you would like. Advertising won't always produce the results you expect or need. Your first years in business might not generate the profit you expect or project. Don't expect immediate gratification from everything that you do. Getting your business to the level of success you desire can be a long process. Stay focused and be patient.

MISTAKES

While it is not a pleasant thought or something that you look forward to, mistakes are inevitable. They are a part of life. As with any other endeavor, you will make bad decisions for the right and wrong reasons. You will make bad decisions because of inexperience. Just remember, mistakes are *opportunities* to learn and grow. If you are smart and a survivor, you will handle them as such.

PAYOFFS, BENEFITS, AND REWARDS

There are more wonderful things about owning a home-based business than I have time or space to talk about. So I've decided to highlight a few that will, I hope, get you motivated to start your home-based baking business.

- You're the *boss*!
- Your work takes place in the comfort and convenience of your home.
- You design a work schedule that suits your personal and business needs. Work can take place early mornings, late nights, or weekends.
- You set company rules and policies.
- No travel time or expense to and from work.
- You have no obligation to stay at home for a certain number of hours each day. You can come and go as you please.
- Very little overhead cost. Only a slight increase in utility bills and the cost of liability insurance coverage if you choose to carry it.
- No additional rent. When your home rent or mortgage is paid, so is your business rent.
- Many tax deductions.
- Total control over your product line: the types of products you offer, flavors, sizes, prices, whether to sell wholesale or retail, types of packaging, where and how the products will be shipped or delivered, and much more.
- The opportunity to try new ideas and show off your creativity.
- The joy, pleasure, excitement, and satisfaction of having people taste your products and enjoy them so much that they become regular customers and refer you to their family, friends, and coworkers.
- The feeling of accomplishment when an upscale restaurant, dessert café, or hotel puts your desserts on their menu or displays them in their dessert case.
- The feeling of reward when the phone rings with your first $500 or $1,000 order.

- Last but not least, *income*! This business is loaded with income potential. The amount of money you make will vary with the amount of time you invest in the business, the types of products you offer, the formula you use for pricing products, the types and sizes of equipment you choose to make the products, your ability to research and purchase items at the best prices, your choice of advertising for the business, your choice of shipping and delivery method(s), cash flow management, and more.

To explain further, let's look at an income scenario: You operate a cookie business. Your cookies sell for $12 a dozen retail. Your average sales are ten dozen cookies a day, five days a week. At this rate, your gross annual sales will be $31,200. Now, your profit from the $31,200 will depend on how well you manage or handle the variables mentioned above. My point is that no one can tell you exactly how much money a business will generate. Income and success will vary. It has been reported that a now-famous food guru made over a million dollars during her first year of catering from home. At the opposite end of the scale, there are reports of $25,000 to $30,000 in annual income from home-based food businesses. Your income will be determined by how hard you work and how much you invest. You're the boss. You're in control. You must set the goals and make them happen.

CHAPTER 2

A LICENSED HOME-BASED BAKING BUSINESS

Imagine opening a door to the perfect workplace in your home. This room is outfitted with all of the necessary equipment and tools for you to create and produce your special baked goods. This great work area also has the important stamp of approval from all of the governing agencies (business license department and health/agriculture department). You have a legitimate business in your home, and you never have to be concerned that a situation will arise that will find you without the proper credentials. To assist you with changing these wonderful images into real life, I've created a guide that starts at the beginning and walks you step by step through the process.

Now, let's start with a very important but not so well-known fact. Not all cities, counties, and health departments issue permits to operate a food preparation business in the home. Municipalities vary in the rules, laws, and requirements. The information in this chapter comes from my experience setting up a commercial kitchen in my home. To give you an idea of what you might encounter while renovating your work area, I've listed the major changes made to my one-car garage to get a health permit and business license and make the space user-friendly. My renovations included: enclosing and sealing the garage door so that it doesn't open; new floor covering (linoleum, which was relatively inexpensive and quick to install); completion of interior walls with sheet rock; installing fluorescent lights and a ceiling fan with light; installing plumbing for a stainless-steel sink and a hand sink; adding an electrical line to accommodate the convection oven; installing a special wall outlet for the convection oven and an additional wall outlet for other appliances like mixer, scale, and sealing iron; and, finally, painting the walls and ceiling with a light-colored, washable paint. The following four-step process should assist you with finding out if your home is adaptable and if the governing agencies in your area will issue you the necessary permits to operate your business from home. These steps are also designed to help you save time and money. So, let's get started.

STEP 1. DESIGNATING YOUR WORK SPACE

Look around your home. Do you have a basement, cellar, garage, carport (must be enclosed), or bonus room that can be converted into a work space? The first requirement for a health permit is that your work space must be totally separate from your personal kitchen. You cannot share use of sinks, ovens, tables, or any other equipment. This means that you need to create a microbakery and kitchen for working. This room will need running water, good lighting, electrical outlets, and proper wiring for commercial equipment. If you do not have such a space available for renovation, you may not be able to obtain a health permit or business license to operate your food business from home. Now, if all of these things seem feasible, move to the next step.

STEP 2. LICENSE AND PERMITS

Call the business license office in your city or county. Explain that you are interested in starting a baking and food business from your home. Also explain that you will be delivering or shipping all products to your customers (see zoning permit). Then ask what the procedure is to get a license for your business. A zoning permit and a permit from the health department might be required before a business license can be issued.

Zoning Department. Some cities and counties have restricted areas for home-based businesses (particularly a food business). If you are issued a zoning permit, expect it to be accompanied by laws and rules, such as no business signage on your house or in the yard, no large delivery trucks bringing supplies (with the exception of the usual delivery companies like UPS, FedEx, etc.), and minimum vehicles at your residence at any one time.

Health Department or Agriculture Department. This department has a list of rules and regulations that must be followed to get a permit. Here are a few requirements you should expect: Your work kitchen must be a room separate from your personal kitchen and must be equipped so that its function is totally independent of your personal kitchen. Walls and floors must be painted or covered with washable materials. Additionally, a commercial stainless-steel compartment sink, a worktable with a nonporous surface (such as stainless steel), a hand sink, and a regulation scale (depending on your product line) might be required.

STEP 3. RENOVATIONS

If you decide to continue after researching steps 1 and 2, you'll need to find licensed, knowledgeable, reputable, and affordable people or companies to do the renovations. If you don't have family, friends, or personal knowledge of someone else in this line of work, you will need to research at least three companies for each project: electrical, plumbing, drywall, floor covering, and painting (if you choose not to do the painting yourself). A great way to find these companies is to ask people that you know and trust for referrals. If you can't get referrals, check the neighborhood paper or the local yellow pages. Whatever approach you decide to take, you'll need to ask lots of questions, make lots of notes, and compare, compare, compare. So get busy with your pad, pen, and queries.

One more suggestion: If you decide that doing business with family or friends is the best and most affordable way to go, make sure all parties have a clear understanding of the work to be done, deadlines, payment, and any other details that might cause problems. You should get estimates in writing, just as you would with any other contractor.

STEP 4. EQUIPMENT AND SUPPLIES

With steps 1 to 3 completed or researched, you're ready for equipment, storage units, tools, small wares, ingredients, packaging, and supplies. Chapters 4 and 5 will assist you with choosing the best and most affordable equipment, small wares, and tools for your business. Chapter 17 will tell you where to find these items plus where to find ingredients, packaging, and supplies.

Here's another work-at-home option: If you have the ground space (land) and the budget allows, you might consider adding a workroom to your existing home. If you decide to do this, *please* check with the zoning department in your city or county first. It's possible that you will need a building permit. Adding a room is a much more involved and expensive process than renovating a room in your home. Therefore, a well-thought-out and written budget is critical to the success of the project. Don't forget the important search for *good* and *affordable* contractors. The same considerations for electricity, gas, plumbing, floor and wall covering mentioned earlier in this chapter will apply to the new room.

Chapter 3

Structure Your Business

1. CHOOSE A NAME FOR THE BUSINESS

Choosing the right name for a business is very important. The name you choose will have a lasting effect (for better or for worse). I've listed a few tips that will, I hope, assist you.

- Avoid using words that might offend others.
- Try not to use words that are long and difficult to spell. Long names can become a problem when answering the phone. Words that are difficult to spell can pose a problem when someone's looking for you in a directory.
- If your business name doesn't indicate exactly what you do, use a subtitle to be more descriptive. Example: "Unique Occasions/*The Gourmet Gift Service.*"
- If you can't think of a name that's different or catchy, the simplest and best name might be one that includes your name. Examples: "Sweets by Cynthia" or "Muffins by Melody."

2. REGISTER YOUR NAME

When you've chosen a business name, it should be registered with the proper local and state officials. If you're not sure which office handles registrations, the local business license office can direct you to the proper place.

3. TO TAX OR NOT TO TAX

You must first decide if your sales transactions will be wholesale, retail, or a combination of both. This will determine whether you should collect taxes on sales. If you don't have a clear understanding of the tax laws that govern your city, county, or state, call the state sales tax office for information.

4. CHOOSE YOUR BUSINESS STRUCTURE

This simply means deciding if the business will be a sole proprietorship, partnership, corporation, or another form. Definitions for these terms can be found on the IRS's Web site (www.irs.gov). Your tax preparer or accountant should also be able to explain each structure and assist you with choosing the right one for your business.

5. INSURANCE COVERAGE

Because you are handling and preparing food for public consumption, you should have product liability insurance. I'm sure this isn't an expense that you look forward to, but it's better to be safe than sorry. For leads on companies that insure home-based businesses, ask family, friends, business associates, and other small-business owners. If the information is not found through these inquiries, check the yellow pages. Most insurance companies list their areas of expertise in their ads.

6. CHOOSE AN ACCOUNTANT, TAX PREPARER, AND ATTORNEY

Some small-business owners prepare their own taxes using computer software, but many people are not comfortable doing this. If you're part of the latter group, you will need a good accountant or tax preparer. You will probably operate the business for years without needing the services of an attorney. On the other hand, you could find yourself in a legal dilemma within the first few months. It's better to have a name and number at hand just in case.

The best way to find professionals in these areas is to seek referrals from business associates, family members, friends, or local associations (like the bar association).

BUSINESS PLAN OUTLINE

More times than not, owners of home-based businesses do not have a well-thought-out, written plan for how their businesses will start and operate. Quite often, failure to create a simple plan causes mistakes and oversights with products, money, valued customers, and more. The following outline was constructed as a guide to help you with writing a business plan for your personal use in the business. The examples used in each section are provided to stimulate your thought process.

1. DESCRIPTION OF THE BUSINESS

Provide a detailed description of your business. For example:

- Paula's Pound Cakes is a full-time, home-based bakery that specializes in all-butter pound cakes. These cakes are made from scratch with fresh, quality, natural ingredients. Paula's Pound Cakes services both the retail and wholesale markets. Our irresistible cakes are available in four mouthwatering flavors and three sizes to accommodate desserts for two or for a crowd. For special occasions, we offer glazed, decorative Bundt pound cakes. We also offer a special-flavor pound cake for the holidays (Thanksgiving and Christmas). Within six months, we plan to package our pound cakes for gifts. Within twelve to eighteen months, we will offer wedding cakes using our wonderful pound cake recipes. We take the worry and hassle out of preparing homemade desserts by providing our customers with quality, all-natural, fresh-baked cakes. In addition to making these spectacular pound cakes, we also deliver Monday through Saturday.

2. REASONS TO START THE BUSINESS

Explain in detail. For example:

- I want to supplement my income.
- My current job will be ending soon, and I'm no longer interested in working for someone else.
- I'm a stay-at-home mom, and I need the convenience of working at home.
- I'm tired of the long commute to and from work.
- I need more control over my schedule and more income.
- I want to show the world how creative I am.

3. START-UP COST

If the money needed for your start-up is not already available, free and clear, discuss in detail how you plan to generate those funds. Will you put aside a certain amount from your current income? Will these funds come from a bank loan, credit cards, or from family and friends? List every expense involved to get your business started. Use estimates when exact amounts are not available. For example:

- Renovations to my work area
- Equipment (mixer, oven, tables, etc.)
- Small wares, tools, and baking pans
- Ingredients and packaging supplies
- License, registrations, permits, and other set-up fees
- Office equipment, fax machine, fax line installation

4. EXPERIENCE AND QUALIFICATIONS

Explain in detail. For example:

- I've baked for years for family, friends, fun, and as a hobby.
- I'm a baker at my current job.
- I've been taking baking classes.
- I don't have any baking experience, but I'm good with other foods. I'm excited and enthusiastic about learning to bake and operating this business.

5. OPERATING PROCEDURES

Discuss in detail. For example:

- Hours of operation. Because this is a home-based business, it is not necessary for me to maintain strict hours or stay at the office to answer the phone. The majority of my orders will be delivered, but when there's a pick-up, I will be at the office. When I'm away from the office, my calls will be handled by the answering service or voice mail. I will call in every hour to check messages. I also have the option of forwarding calls to my cell phone.
- The ordering process. Customers will have three order options: phone, fax, and e-mail. Within four to six months online ordering will also be available.
- Order turnaround time. Small orders (ten cakes or less) will be delivered in twenty-four to forty-eight hours. Larger orders will require additional time, depending on the size of the order.
- Delivery and shipping. I will thoroughly research all delivery and shipping methods available to me and make comparisons. Initially I will make deliveries in my immediate area. This will help with my budget and give me opportunities to meet customers and promote the business. I will choose one of the other options for long-distance shipping and make a test run to make sure the pound cakes will arrive in good condition. If there are problems, I will work to correct them before offering this service to my customers.
- Customer satisfaction. All pound cakes will be sold with a customer satisfaction guarantee. If a customer is unhappy with a purchase,

money will be refunded, except for delivery or shipping charges. This offer will be good only if the customer returns the product.

6. POTENTIAL MARKET

Whom do you visualize as your customers? Discuss in detail. For example:

- Paula's Pound Cakes will be sold wholesale to upscale restaurants, delicatessens, cafés, and caterers. There are ten to twelve of these businesses in my area.
- Paula's Pound Cakes will be sold retail to businesses, organizations, and private clubs for meetings, parties, special events, and gifts.
- Paula's Pound Cakes will also be sold for personal occasions and gifts.

7. MARKETING AND ADVERTISING PLAN

What's your plan for creating interest in your pound cakes and selling them? Explain in detail. For example:

- I will distribute business cards to all of my family, friends, and associates to announce the opening of my business.
- I will have a flyer made that announces the opening of Paula's Pound Cakes. It will describe the cakes, give sizes, flavors, and prices, and tell how to get more information or place an order. I will ask everyone that I know to take a few flyers and give them to people that they know.
- I will purchase two magnet signs for my vehicle.
- I will research and purchase a Web site.
- I will create a press release about the opening of my home-based business and send a press packet to all of the local newspapers, magazines, and radio stations. One of my fresh-baked pound cakes will be included with the information.
- I will become familiar with local networking groups so that I can

attend meetings and promote my company.

- I will look for opportunities to hand out pound cake samples and information.
- I will call local food establishments and set up sales appointments with the owner or manager to show and sample the pound cakes.

8. THE COMPETITION

Research and discuss in detail. For example:

- My local competition is one home-based bakery, two dessert cafés, and one gourmet pastry shop.
- The home-based bakery operates part-time and is unable to respond to everyone in a timely fashion.
- The dessert cafés' products are very pricey, and they do not offer delivery.
- Products at the gourmet pastry shop are lacking in quality. Also, the shop does not offer delivery outside of their immediate area.
- Grocery-store bakeries and club-warehouse bakeries also offer pound cakes. While my pound cakes far exceed theirs in quality, they offer much lower prices. Their products are also easily accessible. In some cases, these stores are open twenty-four hours a day.
- At present, my online competition consists of at least twenty specialty companies. I have not researched all of them or sampled their products. Establishing Paula's Pound Cakes online will take time, patience, and a lot of promoting.

9. CUSTOMER SERVICE

What will you do to service customers, keep them happy, and show appreciation for their business? Discuss in detail. For example:

- Initially, I will call each customer to ask if the products arrived in good condition and if they were pleased with everything.

- As business increases, the follow-up process will change. New customers will receive calls (as many as time permits). Repeat customers will receive a postage-paid survey postcard. Comments and suggestions from the survey will later be posted on my Web site.
- I will send birthday cards to all of my contact people at companies and organizations. This will promote good relations and keep them thinking of Paula's Pound Cakes.

10. EDUCATION

Owning and operating a business requires continuous learning and growth. The Small Business Administration offers useful business classes through community colleges, universities, and community centers. At colleges and universities, these classes are usually offered by the evening studies or continuing education department. Take a look at the course offerings. From the descriptions, choose a class or classes that will assist you most. The classes are relatively inexpensive and the benefits far outweigh the time and money spent.

What are your plans for learning and staying informed? Explain in detail. For example:

- I will take business classes at the community college or the adult community center.
- I plan to take classes on how to bake, decorate, market, and deliver wedding cakes.
- I will subscribe to food industry magazines to stay informed of new products, trends, and changes in the market.

11. GOALS

Where would you like to take Paula's Pound Cakes and at what pace? Explain in detail. The questions below will give you a starting point.

- Where do you see Paula's Pound Cakes in six months?
- How many wholesale accounts will you have at that time?
- What will the average monthly retail sales be?
- Where will Paula's Pound Cakes be in twelve months?
- How many wholesale accounts will you have?
- What will the average monthly retail sales be?
- How many gift cakes would you like to sell for the first holiday season?
- How many wedding cakes would you like to sell on average per month?
- What will your gross sales be in six months?
- What salary amount would you like to take from the business in six months?
- What salary amount would you like to take from the business in twelve months?
- How much profit would you like to clear in six months?
- How much profit would you like to clear in twelve months?

12. ONE-YEAR CASH FLOW PROJECTION STATEMENT

PAULA'S POUND CAKES								September 2006 to August 2007					
	SEP	OCT	NOV	DEC	JAN	FEB	MAR	APR	MAY	JUN	JUL	AUG	TOTAL
Income Sales													
Retail													
Wholesale													
TOTAL SALES													
Expenses													
Post Office													
Postage													
Box Rent													
Delivery													
Courier													
UPS, FedEx													
Other													
Shipping Boxes & Supplies													
Office Supplies													
Advertising													
Business Cards													
Car Magnets													
Flyers													

PAULA'S POUND CAKES					September 2006 to August 2007							
	SEP	OCT	NOV	DEC	JAN	FEB	MAR	APR	MAY	JUN	JUL	AUG	TOTAL
Postcards													
Other													
Communications													
Telephone													
Cell Phone													
Banking													
Bank Service Charges													
Check Printing													
Merchant Account Fee													
Internet													
Monthly Fee													
Merchant Services													
Travel													
Mileage													
Tolls													
Parking													
Meals													
Car Insurance													
Liability Insurance													
Education													

PAULA'S POUND CAKES							September 2006 to August 2007						
	SEP	OCT	NOV	DEC	JAN	FEB	MAR	APR	MAY	JUN	JUL	AUG	TOTAL
Subscriptions													
Trade Magazines													
Books/ Software													
Utilities													
Inventory													
Ingredients													
Packaging													
Loan Payment													
Paula's Salary													
Other													
Other													
TOTAL EXPENSES													
**PROFIT													

*This outline was set up for an example only. You should make changes in categories and other information to fit your business.

**Subtract total income from total expenses.

Chapter 4

Baking Equipment

My mission in this chapter is to give you a feel for the kind of equipment that's usually required by the health department, equipment not required but needed, and where the equipment can be purchased. I've included a few helpful tips that can make your work a little easier and less time consuming. There are also tips on equipment that's traditionally used in a personal kitchen but can also be used in your business to get you started.

Here's your first money-saving tip: used commercial equipment will more than satisfy your needs. It's not necessary to purchase new equipment. Commercial equipment tends to have a long operating life when it's taken care of properly.

The following equipment list will be especially helpful if you're operating on a shoestring budget. It will also be helpful if you don't have budget issues but are uncertain about operating this type of business and want to test the waters.

OVENS

The health department has no requirements concerning the size, type, or make of oven you use, only that you have one in your work area. You can use the same type of conventional stove that you have in your personal kitchen if it bakes properly and produces the results that you need. But you should be aware that conventional ovens limit the quantity that you can bake at one time and the speed of the baking. If you have a large order and a short time frame, the conventional oven will most definitely be a problem.

Here's one of my experiences with the conventional oven. Not long after starting my business, a friend helped me get a project with one of the locally based airlines. This project involved baking sheet cakes for a Founder's Day celebration. The airline was giving cake and punch to everyone who came through the gates from morning to afternoon. When my friend asked if I would like to do this, of course I said yes. Being excited about the offer and thinking about the amount of money I could make, I forgot about my baking limitations. At the time, I was still using a regular-size kitchen oven. Also, my friend had promised them that the cakes would be fresh-baked from scratch. In short, baking turned into an out-of-control experience. The airline was sending a van every hour to pick up cakes. It was impossible for me to keep up, so they had to wait each time. Needless to say, I was very glad when that day ended. Since that experience, I always stop to consider how much I can successfully accomplish in a certain period of time before I make a commitment. I'm not telling this story to discourage you but only to point out potential problems ahead of time.

If you want to increase production beyond what can be done with a conventional oven, inquire about a home-style convection stove. This stove is called "fast bake" by some manufacturers. It doesn't necessarily hold a larger quantity of product, but it does bake faster. Call home appliance stores in your area for more information. Also, make sure they understand that you're looking for a stove with *convection baking.*

Commercial ovens are commonly referred to as convection ovens. If your specialty is baking, a commercial convection oven is exactly what you need. Convection baking is much faster than traditional baking and much more efficient. Here's how it works: a fan inside the oven circulates heat so there are no hot or cool spots; therefore, your product bakes faster and more evenly without the need for rotating pans. Commercial convection ovens bake about 25 percent faster than conventional ovens and are available in gas and electric. They are usually referred to as half size and full size. Half-size ovens (one door) will usually hold four to six half-sheet pans (18 × 13 inches) and full-size ovens (two doors) will usually hold four to six full-sheet pans (18 × 26 inches). See the "Where to Find It" chapter under "Baking

Equipment and Tools" for sources of new and used convection ovens. Before purchasing a commercial electric oven, inquire about wiring and outlets needed for operation. Before purchasing any type of gas oven, make sure you have enough space for a hood fan and proper ventilation.

MIXERS

If you have budget concerns, the home-style stand mixer will work perfectly to get you started. I suggest investing in a KitchenAid mixer, if you don't already have one. KitchenAid manufactures high quality, heavy-duty mixers that are very dependable and get the job done more efficiently than many other stand mixers. Bowl sizes range from four to six quarts. KitchenAid mixers are often available on sale at discount and department stores. Take a little time to shop and compare for the best deal. If you have the product demand and the budget, definitely invest in a commercial mixer. A used commercial mixer will get you off to a great start. Twelve-quart, twenty-quart, and thirty-quart mixers are the most popular sizes for a start-up small business. See the "Where to Find It" chapter under "Baking Equipment and Tools" for sources of new and used commercial mixers. In the same chapter, you will find contact information for the KitchenAid Company, which also offers refurbished mixers with warranties.

REFRIGERATORS

Are you watching the budget? If so, here's another tip that will save you many dollars. Home-style refrigerators will work perfectly for your start-up and established business. When I started my business, I didn't have the money to purchase a refrigerator, so I rented one from a rent-to-own company. I continued to rent until eventually I owned it. I am very happy to say that my first refrigerator is still working perfectly and I still use it. I'm telling this rental story to make a point: There are workable alternatives. You don't have to buy all commercial equipment (new or used) to get a great start. Also, renting additional refrigeration is a practical idea for peak seasons such as Valentine's Day, Thanksgiving, and Christmas. It's the perfect quick-fix for a limited budget or lack of cash flow. The health department isn't concerned about the size or make of your refrigerator. They are only interested in the fact that you have one in your work area. Depending on your needs, two used, home-style refrigerators might cost less than one commercial refrigerator. Commercial refrigerators (referred to as coolers) start with the one-door size and increase by numbers of doors and dimensions of the doors. Coolers, even used ones, can be expensive, so consider carefully the amount of space you have, the amount of product to be chilled, and your budget for refrigeration. Before purchasing a commercial cooler, inquire about the necessary electrical wiring and outlets needed for operation. For sources of new and used coolers, see the "Where to Find It" chapter under "Baking Equipment and Tools."

PROOFING CABINETS

If you're making large quantities of yeast breads, you will benefit from having a proofing cabinet. This cabinet maintains a warm temperature that's perfect for the stage of bread making when the dough needs to rise and double in bulk. See the "Where to Find It" chapter under "Baking Equipment and Tools" for sources of new and used proofing cabinets.

SINKS

A stainless-steel compartment sink is usually a requirement of the health department. Even if this type of sink is not required, get one if you can afford it. The convenience and ease of washing large sheet pans, large mixing bowls, and other oversized pieces make it well worth the cost. Commercial stainless-steel sinks range in size from two to four compartments, with optional drain boards. See the "Where to Find It" chapter under "Baking Equipment and Tools" for sources of new and used compartment sinks.

WORK TABLES

The health department usually requires a certain kind of work surface for food preparation and protection. Stainless-steel tables are the most popular because they can be easily cleaned and do not absorb germs and other contaminants. There may be other tabletop surfaces that meet approval. Ask your health department for more information. The size of table you buy should be determined by available space and the task to be performed.

Don't forget to measure your space before you buy. See the "Where to Find It" chapter under "Baking Equipment and Tools" for sources of new and used work tables.

ROLLING PAN RACKS (SHELVES)

There's no need to purchase new pan racks. These heavy-duty metal racks are made to hold both half- and full-size sheet pans. They vary in height and the number of pans they hold. They are excellent space savers. Use them for cookies and cakes (before and after baking), ingredients, supplies, and more. One of the great convenience features is mobility. They can be moved to wherever you're working. A pan rack is not required by the health department, but it should be near the top of your list of necessities. See the "Where to Find It" chapter under "Baking Equipment and Tools" for sources of new and used rolling pan racks.

STORAGE SHELVES

You will need lots of storage space for dry ingredients, packaging supplies, and other items. It's always a great idea to make the most of your work space from floor to ceiling. So here's another space-saving, budget-friendly idea: purchase one or two (depending on available space) heavy-duty, plastic utility shelf units from a local building supply store such as Home Depot or Lowe's. Most units come with five very sturdy, durable shelves. The shelves are continuously stackable so you can purchase additional units and create a set of six or seven shelves (space permitting). Don't shy away from purchasing this type of shelf unit because it's made of plastic. I've used several of them in my work area for many years, sometimes putting 50 pounds or more on one shelf. If you're interested in commercial chrome/wire shelf units, they can be found at restaurant supply stores, building supply stores, Sam's Club, and Costco Wholesale. For more information on new and used commercial units, see the "Where to Find It" chapter under "Baking Equipment and Tools."

HAND SINK

A hand sink is generally a small sink used to wash your hands before and during work. This sink is usually required by the health department. There's no need to purchase a new or used commercial hand sink. You can save on cost by purchasing a fiberglass sink (called a utility sink) at most building supply stores. See the "Where to Find It" chapter under "Baking Equipment and Tools" for new and used commercial hand sinks.

INGREDIENT BINS

It's not necessary to buy commercial storage bins for items like flour and sugar. Just go to a building supply store and purchase some large thirty-two-gallon trash cans with lids. *They must be new, of course.* These cans will store a fifty-pound bag of flour or sugar and more. But do not empty the product directly into the trash can. Instead, drop the unopened bag into the trash can, and then open the top of the bag and dip out the product as needed. These cans also fit conveniently under most work tables, saving precious work space. I've used this type of storage since the beginning of my business. If you find it necessary to use commercial storage bins, they are available both new and used. See the "Where to Find It" chapter under "Baking Equipment and Tools."

TIPS:

If you know people in the food business, ask them for a suggestion of a good used-equipment company.

Before purchasing used equipment like refrigerators, freezers, ovens, or mixers, have the salesperson turn them on. Don't purchase without knowing that the equipment will run.

Before purchasing any large equipment, measure all doorways that the equipment has to pass through before it can be placed in the work area. If any equipment is too large to clear the door opening, you will be forced to remove the door frame (and maybe more) or let the delivery company take the equipment back. Either option could be inconvenient and costly.

Always ask for a warranty. Most companies offer at least a thirty-day warranty on used equipment.

CHAPTER 5

SMALL WARES AND TOOLS

The items listed below are only a few of the things that will be needed to operate your business. In my experience, these tools are essential to maintaining consistency, quality, and professionalism.

BAKING PANS

Choose the bakeware that works best for your products. The type of pans you use will affect the taste, texture, size, and appearance of your products. You'll want to use pans that bake evenly and resist sticking or burning. Lightweight pans sometimes bake unevenly and burn the product before it's done. Using pans that are too dark can also result in burned product. The ideal baking pan for cookies is the commercial-style "half-sheet" or "full-sheet" pan. The half sheet bakes twelve or eighteen cookies, depending on the cookie size. It will fit in any conventional home-style oven. The full sheet bakes double the amount and will only fit in a commercial or oversized oven. If you're starting a brownie business, these sheet pans will be perfect. However, if you're making very thick brownies, the sides of the sheet pans might not be high enough. Making cheesecakes? You have many options: traditional springform pans; solid-bottom, high-wall pans (usually three inches deep); cupcake tins for mini cheesecakes; and more. You're only limited by your creativity.

If you're considering pound cakes as a specialty, there's everything from the traditional tube pan, the original Bundt pan, the theme-designed Bundt pans, the mini-Bundt pans, to loaf pans (regular and mini size). If you or your customers will be slicing the pound cake for resale, the traditional tube pan or loaf pan is the best choice. This way you have total control of the number of slices the cake will yield without having to work around special designs or portioned segments. If your cakes are going to the destination whole, as a gift or to be used in a personal setting, consider using the more decorative Bundt pans. Themes and designs add a lot of excitement and flair to the cake. The majority of my baking pans were purchased from Parrish's Supplies. This company carries an excellent line of commercial-quality products. I'm still using pans that I purchased more than twelve years ago, and they still bake like new. See the "Where to Find It" chapter under "Baking Equipment and Tools" for Parrish's and other companies that sell retail and wholesale.

CAKE TURNTABLE

A turntable (carousel) makes frosting and decorating cakes much easier, faster, and smoother. An inexpensive turntable can be purchased from most discount stores. A heavier, more professional type can be found at cake decorating stores, hobby and crafts stores, Wilton Enterprises, or wholesale suppliers. See the "Where to Find It" chapter under "Baking Equipment and Tools."

COOKIE SCOOPS

If you decide to offer cookies in your product line, a cookie scoop is an item that you shouldn't be without. Using a scoop keeps your cookies consistent in size. Unless you're selling cookies by weight, size consistency is very important for pricing purposes. Cookie scoops look like ice-cream scoops, just smaller. They can be purchased in many sizes at bakery or restaurant supply stores. They are labeled or stamped with a number to designate the size. See the "Where to Find It" chapter under "Baking Equipment and Tools."

FOOD PROCESSOR

Are you making, or planning to make, anything with shredded or grated vegetables like carrots, chopped nuts, chopped apples, or similar ingredients? If so, you'll benefit greatly from having a food processor. If you are new to the business, you will soon realize that labor is a critical and lengthy part of getting your products to market. Any equipment or tool that you can use to cut labor time is a great investment. Food processors are relatively inexpensive and can be found at local discount stores. I recommend that you skip the small, one-cup processor and purchase at least a four-cup processor. If you're interested in a larger, more professional-type processor, check out restaurant equipment or bakery supply stores. See the "Where to Find It" chapter under "Baking Equipment and Tools."

MEASURING CUPS AND SPOONS

Always use standard measuring tools to ensure consistency in your products. The cups and spoons from your tableware are not accurate measuring tools. You will need a liquid measuring cup, a set of dry/solid measuring cups, and standard measuring spoons. Liquid measuring cups are usually see-through and look like little pitchers with measurements printed on the sides. Dry measuring cups come in graduated sizes and must have smooth, unbroken rims, making it possible to level off overflow. Standard measuring spoons come in sets and always include graduated sizes, from one-fourth teaspoon to one tablespoon. These items can be found in most discount, bakery supply, and restaurant supply stores.

SPATULAS

You will need a good rubber spatula for scraping mixing bowls. If you're frosting cakes, you'll need at least one metal spatula. The sizes you purchase should be determined by the size of the mixing bowls that you're using, the size and height of the cakes you're frosting, and how comfortable the spatulas are in your hand when using them. Both types of spatulas can be found at discount stores, cake decorating stores, bakery supply stores, and restaurant supply stores.

FOOD SCALE

If a recipe calls for chocolate by weight, you'll need a scale, particularly if you purchase by the case or ten-pound slab. If you decide to package and sell specialty nuts, pretzels, or candy, you will need an accurate scale for weighing. As business and production increase, you might prefer to weigh ingredients rather than measure them, to maintain consistency. There are many uses for a good scale. For accuracy, I suggest purchasing a digital scale. It's an investment you won't regret. See the "Where to Find It" chapter under "Baking Equipment and Tools."

DOUBLE BOILER

Will you have a need for melted chocolate? Will you be making cooked frostings like the "seven-minute frosting"? Will any of your recipes call for slow heating or cooking of ingredients? If so, a double boiler is a must. A starter size can be found at discount and department stores. For commercial sizes, see the "Where to Find It" chapter under "Baking Equipment and Tools."

CAKE AND PIE MARKERS

If you're selling cakes or pies by the slice, or if you're selling whole cakes or pies that need to be pre-marked or portioned, these markers will be very helpful. They are available in several different portion sizes. They can be purchased from restaurant or bakery supply stores. See the "Where to Find It" chapter under "Baking Equipment and Tools."

BROWNIE CUTTERS

If brownies are your specialty or a part of your product line, you'll need a fast, accurate, and consistent way to cut them. I've faced the task of cutting many pans of brownies at one time, and it can be very time consuming and inaccurate if you don't have a size guide for cutting. Your ultimate concern should be your customer. Whether your sales are retail or wholesale, the customer expects and should get consistency. Brownie cutters can be purchased in different sizes, depending on the pan size and the brownie portion that you need. See the "Where to Find It" chapter under "Baking Equipment and Tools."

HEAT SEALER

Properly sealed packaging says that you're concerned about food safety, quality, and freshness. It also says you're concerned about the appearance of your product. A heat sealer is relatively inexpensive when you consider the long-term use and the value added to your product. See the "Where to Find It" chapter under "Gift Packaging Equipment."

CAKE DECORATING KIT

If you want your cakes, cupcakes, and other pastries to look like the fancy gourmet desserts in magazines or upscale stores, you'll need basic decorating supplies like a pastry bag and a few decorating tips (metal or plastic). These items can be found at most discount, hobby, craft, and cake decorating stores. If you've never done simple cake decorations, there is a special kit that you can buy ("Decorating 101"). This kit not only has the necessary basic tools, such as pastry bags and decorating tips, it also contains a practice board with illustrations of simple but elegant decorations. If you need help beyond the illustration board, there are videos for the beginner. You can find sources for the decorating kit and videos in the "Where to Find It" chapter under "Cake Decorating Supplies."

BAKERY BOXES AND BOARDS

It's difficult to operate any baking business without packaging for your products. Even if you're not interested in packaging for gifts, you'll still need items like basic white bakery boxes, cake boards, and bags. These items can be found at cake decorating stores and hobby or craft stores in small quantities at retail prices. Food wholesalers and food container companies carry them in case quantities (your best buy). If you're looking for fancy decorative bakery boxes, they are available from the Hubert Company. To personalize and create name recognition, inexpensively, you can stamp basic white bakery boxes or solid color bags with a custom rubber stamp, or you can have custom labels printed with your company's name, your specialty, phone number, and other contact information. Custom labels are available in many colors including gold and silver metallic. A custom label will give your otherwise plain bakery boxes and bags a classy, upscale look. Now, if you have a little more to spend, you can have the packaging (boxes and bags) custom printed with your company name, logo, phone number, address, and more. This type of printing usually requires that you purchase a minimum of one thousand boxes or bags. Research and compare before making a purchase. Information on the Hubert Company and other packaging wholesalers can be found in the "Where to Find It" chapter under "Bakery Packaging and Supplies"; companies that offer custom labels can be found under "Put Your Stamp on It." Office supply stores, printing companies, and business service companies can provide you with a custom rubber stamp.

Chapter 6

Alternatives to Baking At Home

If you don't have the proper space in your home or you're unable to meet the requirements of the city or health department, here are a few budget-friendly alternatives that might help you get the business started outside of your home. None of these ideas require the traditional renting or leasing of retail space. Consider approaching the following companies and organizations with your dilemma. They might be willing to share space with you at a low start-up cost and reasonable monthly rates until you're able to get a place of your own.

If you're able to work out an agreement with someone to share space, don't forget to put the agreement in writing. This agreement can be something very simple that outlines your working hours, use of the store's equipment, storage space for ingredients and supplies, bartering, if any, and the total cost of overhead. Don't forget signatures and dates. Written agreements can serve as friendly reminders to all parties involved.

RESTAURANTS

Restaurants that have a little extra working space or need additional operating funds might be willing to rent kitchen space and equipment during regular hours or after the restaurant closes. Restaurants usually have equipment (like mixers and commercial convection ovens) that you will most likely need to make your products. The use of their kitchen and equipment would mean much lower start-up and operating costs for you. Talk with the owner or manager about your situation. Explain where you are with your business, what your needs are, and what you're trying to accomplish. This type of start-up has been successful for many well-known businesses. Tip: If you plan to bake a product that the restaurant can use, try to trade product for overhead cost.

CATERERS

Many caterers have the kind of equipment that you will need for baking. You might be able to trade product for overhead in this situation.

CHURCHES

Churches quite often have commercial kitchens used to prepare food for gatherings and other events. Perhaps the church could use some of your products for fund-raisers in exchange for overhead. This might also give you an opportunity to reach the church membership: *a great marketing opportunity*!

INCUBATORS

This is an option that might not be as easy or affordable as the previous three, but it's a fantastic support system and one of the best ways to start a small business if you need assistance. Like incubators for newborn babies, an incubator for small businesses is a facility and a group of people brought together to nurture and support a new business until it's able to function on its own. Business incubators can provide necessities such as clerical services, assistance with business plans, work space, equipment, and other types of support. The purpose of the incubator is to accelerate growth while allowing entrepreneurs the time required to focus on their specialties. Small-business incubators are funded by public, private, and government sources. Be aware that there is usually an admissions process, which can include financial qualifications, a business plan, and more. To find out more about small-business incubators visit the Web site of the National Business Incubator Association (www.nbia.org). You might also inquire at the chamber of commerce, the business license office, or the SBA in your area to find out if there's an incubator near you.

CONTRACT BAKERS

This is an idea that has worked wonderfully for many people but turned into a nightmare for others. Contract bakers are people or companies that use your recipes to make products for you. They can be as small as a local bakery that has just one or two small commercial ovens or as large as a manufacturing company that has a facility with equipment capable of producing hundreds or thousands of products a day. Let's say you have a product that you have perfected and want to put on the market, but you're not interested in making it yourself. Or perhaps you want to make the product but don't have the proper facility. You can contract someone else to make the product for you. If you are currently making products but have outgrown your work space, and if you're not interested in operating a larger facility, there are bakers who will make the product for you. But be careful: this kind of agreement requires a lot of research to find the right person or company, a lot of planning, quite often a substantial amount of funds, and good legal advice to make sure that your interest is protected.

I have personal knowledge of someone who developed a product that was beginning to show promise, but she was not in a position to set up a home-based bakery or open a retail store. She decided to approach one of her current restaurant customers with the idea of making the product for her. She and the restaurant owner reached a workable agreement, or so she thought. The agreement simply stated that the restaurant would use her recipes to make product for *her* business. It would not be involved in any business decisions related to her products or company. This arrangement didn't work for very long. The restaurant owner began to make changes to the products and took over decision making that should have been left to the product owner. The restaurant also started to make and sell products without the owner's permission. Needless to say, she discontinued the agreement and walked away very disappointed. There are many stories similar to this one where the contract company started to use the owner's product and put its name on the packaging. Finding the right company to make your product is critical to the success of the venture. If you feel that this is a workable plan for you, take your time, do your homework, get legal advice, and take as many preventive measures as possible. Also ask yourself this important question: How do I feel about turning over my recipes to another company? There are many companies enjoying great success from working with contract bakers. According to a popular TV program *Recipe for Success* on the Food Network, a pound cake company, a banana bread company, a cookie company, and many others have been very successful using contract bakers.

CHAPTER 7

WHAT'S YOUR SPECIALTY?

FAVORITE RECIPES

Do you have a favorite recipe that you've made for many years, and each time you make it your family and friends tell you how great it is? Does this favorite seem to get better each time you make it? This could very easily be your specialty. And chances are, with a little fine tuning, this favorite could be introduced to the market.

THE SEARCH FOR A SPECIAL PRODUCT

Are you interested in baking but don't have a special product? I've dedicated a chapter in this manual to recipes. Some have been used in my business, and others have been used for personal events and special occasions. If you don't see anything in the recipe section that piques your interest, try browsing through cookbooks. Some of my favorite recipes come from the *Southern Living* cookbooks. They can be found at most bookstores and libraries, and also at Oxmoor House Books, which you can find online at www.oxmoorhouse.com or by calling 205-877-6560.

CREATING YOUR PRODUCT LINE

When creating your product line, *keep it simple*. Don't try to be all things to all people. This is something I learned the hard way. The fewer items you offer, the less space you will need for inventory. There's usually not a lot of usable space when you dedicate part of your home to a business. The fewer items you offer, the less money you'll need to stock or restock inventory. For example, if you offer ten items and three or four are slow sellers, the special ingredients in those slow-selling products, which you probably purchased in bulk, are just sitting on the shelf, not being used, not generating sales, and possibly spoiling. This is a waste of space and money. Also, the time and cost to pick up or have ingredients delivered for those slow-selling products will affect your cash flow and eventually your profit. The fewer items you offer, the less money you'll need to spend on marketing and advertising materials. If you make the world's best chocolate chip cookie, you can advertise it on a full-color postcard in detail with room to spare. Whatever the specialty, you don't have to offer a dozen flavors to be successful. For example, Famous Amos, as we all know, started and became famous with a chocolate chip cookie. Nonnie Waller's Traditional Southern, a company that makes Southern pound cakes, offered only two cake flavors for years (www.nonniestraditional.com). Fat Witch Bakery specializes in brownies and, after many years in business, offers just eight flavors (www.fatwitch.com). Yam Good Pies offers only two pie flavors (www.oulalasweets.com). A Couple of Nuts is a specialty nut company that has for several years offered only two flavors of nuts. These companies have been successful focusing on a limited line of specialty products.

COOKIE DOUGH

What about a cookie dough business? Many companies have become very successful making and selling cookie dough. In this business, you would mix the dough, package it in containers (probably plastic tubs or buckets), and keep it refrigerated or frozen until it's shipped or delivered. There are many restaurants, delis, caterers, and hotels that need fresh-baked cookies.

They are usually looking for homemade or gourmet cookie dough that can be baked as needed. Keep in mind that there will not be a need for ovens in this business; however, there will be a demand for more refrigerators or freezers. Another consideration is how to transport the cookie dough and keep it chilled or frozen until it reaches the destination. If this sounds like the business for you, do a lot of research and comparisons before you spend any money.

GOURMET POPCORN

While we're on the subject of specialties, I can't resist suggesting a gourmet popcorn business. I'm talking about made-from-scratch, buttery, yummy, delicious, gourmet popcorn. To my knowledge, there are precious few companies that make really good popcorn. Garrett Popcorn Shops in Chicago sell some of the *best* popcorn you've ever tasted (www.garrettpopcorn.com). They mix two of the most unlikely flavors, caramel and cheddar cheese. Perhaps this sounds strange and unappetizing, but it's just the opposite. This pairing of flavors is unbelievably rich, scrumptious, and unforgettable. A gourmet popcorn business can be as easy to set up and operate as a baking business. The cost for equipment shouldn't be any more expensive than equipment for a baking business. If you don't have recipes for glazing and coating the popcorn, your first tasks will be researching, testing, and creating great recipes. You will also need to search for the best popping corn. To get an idea of equipment needs and costs, check out this Web site: www.popcornmachinesdirect.com. Other equipment and supply companies can be found on the Internet. Use search words like "popcorn machines" or "popcorn supplies." Also check your yellow pages under "Popcorn Equipment" or "Popcorn Supplies."

If you like the food business but you're not interested in baking or making your own products, see the following chapter for ideas.

Chapter 8

Not Interested in Baking but You Love the Food Business?

Consider these ideas ...

Gift-Packaged Specialty Nuts and Snacks

Specialty nuts are always great sellers for my company at holiday time. It takes very little time to weigh, package, seal, and tie on a ribbon. The profit is great and you don't need lots of working space or expensive equipment to operate the business.

Begin by locating companies that make and wholesale specialty nuts. Call them and ask for samples. Most companies will gladly send samples if you introduce yourself with a company name. Compare tastes, flavors, grading (whole nuts or pieces), prices, and shipping costs. Make your selections from the best of these categories. By the way, my best-selling flavors have been cinnamon-spiced pecans, praline pecans, and white-chocolate-covered pecans. You should also consider adding other snack items. Milk-chocolate pretzels, white-chocolate pretzels, and yogurt pretzels are good profit makers. I suggest purchasing all of these items in bulk (by the case). That way your profit margin will be greater. The most popular gift-bag sizes are six, eight, twelve, and sixteen ounces. Stand-alone specialty nut and snack gifts are very popular for personal and small-business gifts. Sources for wholesale nuts and pretzels are in the "Where to Find It" chapter under "Wholesale

Gourmet Foods."

Next, choose your packaging. Cello bags are the most popular and affordable for gift packaging. Heavyweight cello bags are available with designs or themes for almost every holiday and special occasion. These decorative bags add excitement and dollar value to the gift. To maintain consistency in your packaging, use an accurate scale for weighing. For safety and freshness, always use a heat-sealing iron to close the package. Don't forget to attach a card or label describing the contents. Sources for cello bags and heat-sealing irons are in the "Where to Find It" chapter under "Gift Packaging Sources" and "Gift Packaging Equipment."

Other packaging ideas for nuts and snacks are decorative tins, baskets, and gift boxes. If you decide to use tins or gift boxes, use clear cello bags. Decorative cello bags would be an unnecessary expense. If you choose baskets, design or theme bags will add a decorative touch. You can easily increase your profit on these gift items by adding a small package of gourmet coffee, cappuccino, hot chocolate, herbal tea, or a chocolate spoon. See the "Where to Find It" chapter under "Gift Packaging Sources" and "Wholesale Gourmet Foods." For a special touch, offer a personalized gift card with each item. You can use florist-type cards and write the message; or if you have time and access to a computer, you can create professional, personalized cards. For an extra special touch for commercial customers, add their company logo to the cards (you should charge extra for logos).

Not interested in doing your own packaging? You can purchase a variety of specialty nuts and other snack items at wholesale prices that are already gift packaged. This saves both time and the expense of special packaging equipment. Your tasks at this point are to label the bag, if necessary, with a description of the contents, add a gift card, if requested, and add a mark-up for your profit (usually 75 to 100 percent).

Keep in mind, buying prepackaged items might limit your choice of gift-bag designs. See the "Where to Find It" chapter under "Wholesale Gourmet Foods."

GIFT BASKETS ~ YOUR CREATIONS

Making gift baskets can be a very interesting, creative, and profitable business. But there's much, much more to a gift-basket business than putting a few items in a container or basket at holiday time or for special occasions. Gift baskets should be attractively arranged so that items are visible, professionally packed, and well designed. If you're expecting repeat business, referrals, and growth, you need to know many things: your potential market, the products that are most popular with the people you're trying to reach, how to set your prices, how early you should start in order to have a successful holiday or special event, the dos and don'ts of marketing to business and corporate clients (some products are inappropriate for business gifts), how to close a sale after the initial contact is made, and much, much more. If you're interested in a home-based gift-basket business, but you're not sure where to start, how to start, where to find the supplies that you need, how to assemble the baskets, how to price the baskets, who will buy your baskets, or how to market your baskets, you're in luck. There are seasoned professionals in the gift-basket industry who can answer all of these questions. In particular, the magazine *Rave Reviews* does an excellent job assisting both new and existing basket businesses. This magazine features useful tips to get you started and keep you on track, articles and instructions by professionals, photos of professionally made baskets, seasonal how-tos, industry calendars that keep you updated on special events, sources for gift basket supplies, the latest tricks of the trade, and more. If you're interested in creating gift baskets, a subscription to *Rave Reviews* is well worth the cost; to subscribe, call 888-728-3101 or visit their Web site at www.ravereviewsmag. com. Cherie Reagor, the creator of *Rave Reviews*, also offers a series of how-to videos on gift-basket making and more; for more information, visit www. cheriereagor.com. Shirley Frazier, another well-known and experienced gift-basket specialist, has written several how-to books that are available on Amazon.com. Research all of these sources. You'll find a wealth of information.

PREMADE GIFT BASKETS

There are wholesale companies that specialize in premade gift baskets. These baskets are available in many different themes, designs, and sizes. All of the work is done for you. Your task is to market and advertise the baskets, take orders, then call the basket company to place the order. When the baskets arrive, you might need to fluff the bows a little; otherwise, they're ready for delivery to your customers. This is a great business if you're not interested in purchasing and operating equipment to create products. This business involves little overhead. See the "Where to Find It" chapter under "Gourmet Gift Sets."

PROFESSIONAL CAKE DECORATING

Do you like decorating cakes but don't particularly care for the baking process? Do you think you would enjoy cake decorating, but you've never tried it? There are companies, large and small, that hire people just to decorate cakes. Many caterers, restaurants, grocery stores, and small businesses have the know-how to bake a great cake but don't have the time or experience to decorate, nor do they have the budget to hire a full-time, experienced person to do the work. If you're not interested in working for a company as an employee, you can offer your cake decorating services as a contractor. This means that you will be called as a specialist when the company needs your services (weddings, birthdays, etc.). You own and operate the business, set your own prices, control your schedule, and say yes or no to job offers. You're in control. The more creative and experienced you are, the greater your income. If this sounds interesting, do a little research. Check in your area for anyone that makes decorated cakes. Find out if they have a cake decorator on the payroll. Talk with the owner or manager to get a feel for whether they're happy with the work that this person is doing. If you have photos of your work, prepare a portfolio and take it with you to appointments or interviews. Being a contract decorator means owning a business with very little start-up cost and relatively low overhead.

If you don't know how to decorate, but you think professional cake decorating would be a good career or business, you have several educational opportunities. Many cake-decorating supply stores, hobby and craft stores (such as Michaels and Hobby Lobby), community centers, and community colleges (with evening programs) offer cake-decorating classes. There are also books and videos dedicated to the subject. Wilton, a well-known company in the cake-decorating industry, offers a great selection of how-to books and videos. For more information, call 1-800-794-5866 or visit their Web site at www.wilton.com. Again, do the necessary research to make an informed decision. Happy decorating and have fun!

CHAPTER 9

FROM GOURMET TO GIFT

It's so easy to turn your fabulous desserts and creations into elegantly packaged gourmet gifts. To accomplish this, you need to know where to find gift packaging and how to choose appropriately for business gifts, personal gifts, and other special occasions. Once you have the right packaging, knowing how to combine product with packaging is the key to producing tasteful, beautiful gifts. The amount you would usually charge for an item can be increased substantially when it's gift packaged. Offering gourmet gifts is a great opportunity to increase your income and customer base.

INSIDE PACKAGING

Professional, elegant gift packaging starts on the inside of the package. You'll need to learn how to package so that your product is protected. There are several different methods and materials that can be used. It's impossible to discuss all of them in detail, so here is an overview that includes a few tips and suggestions. As your business progresses, take a little time to research and try out different packaging ideas.

When creating inside packaging, your concerns should be appearance and freshness, as well as protection from tampering, germs, extreme weather conditions, or possible mishandling during delivery or shipping. The most popular types of inside packaging are quality, food-approved cello bags, restaurant-quality food-service film, shrink bags, and shrink-wrap. If you feel that your products require custom packaging, there are companies that specialize in finding or creating exactly what you need. See the "Where to

Find It" chapter under "Bakery Packaging and Supplies."

For cookies, brownies, muffins, and breads, I suggest using quality, food-approved cello bags, sealed with a sealing iron. Your products will stay fresh and the package will look professional. For pound cakes, restaurant-quality food-service film or cello products will work well. For pies, shrink-wrap might be best. Shrink-wrapping pies will help to keep the crust from cracking and breaking. For cheesecakes, food-service film or shrink-wrap will work. If the cheesecake has a soft topping, it might be best to freeze first and then wrap. Shrink-wrapping can easily be achieved by using shrink film on the roll or shrink bags and a professional heat gun. To cut cost, a *new* blow-dryer can be used instead of the professional heat gun. For sanitary reasons, this hair dryer should be used in your work area only. See the "Where to Find It Chapter" under "Gift Packaging Sources."

GIFT CONTAINERS

When it comes to gift containers, you have hundreds of choices. There are decorative cello bags, solid color and theme-designed tote bags, solid-color gift boxes, theme-designed gift boxes, baskets in many shapes, sizes, styles, and colors, tins in solid colors and theme designs, decorative cookie jars, and many nontraditional gift containers. You're limited only by your imagination.

CUSTOM GIFT CONTAINERS

If you're looking for something different, something a bit more special and personalized, there are companies that offer custom packaging. You choose the containers, the sizes, the colors, and any graphics. They will make your packaging dreams come to life. However, these companies usually require a percentage of the cost up front and high minimums for production. There could be other fees, such as a plate charge, color match, or setup. Do your research. Ask lots of questions and compare, compare, compare. I've listed several companies in the "Where to Find It" chapter under "Gift Packaging Sources" that carry all of the necessary items to create festive and professional gifts for your customers including custom packaging. If you're not sure how professionally, gift-packaged gourmet desserts look, check out the companies listed below. They are among the most successful gourmet gift companies in the country. Visit their Web sites or call to request a catalog.

Cheryl & Co.
1-800-443-8124
Web site: www.cherylandco.com

Nonnie Waller's Traditional Southern
1-800-664-0919
Web site: www.nonniestraditional.com

Harry & David
1-800-547-3033
Web site: www.harryanddavid.com

MORE GIFT IDEAS

Here are a couple of suggestions that can increase the value of your gifts with little extra work.

Party in a box. This is a great idea for birthday or anniversary gifts. If you're making cakes, particularly pound cakes, consider adding a few items such as candles, decorative napkins, paper plates, forks, party horns, and hats. These items should coordinate or match. Also add a plastic cake cutter, if available. Place the cake and all of the complimentary items in a large gift box (white hat boxes are great for this), tie it with colorful ribbons, tie a big bow on top, and add a balloon (or two). For an added surprise, instead of tying balloons to the outside of the gift box, place a Mylar balloon inside the box so that it automatically comes out when the top is lifted. This is called "party in a box" because everything is included to celebrate and enjoy a great dessert. The same can be done using a nice wicker basket instead of the hat box. Just make sure you pack the bottom of the basket well so that the items are visible and attractively arranged. In this case, the balloons would be tied to the top of the basket. Note that the cake should be individually wrapped or packaged before placing it in the hat box or basket.

Add balloons anytime. Balloons add a festive look and feel to your package. Whether it's a business or personal celebration, your customers will appreciate the option. Until you're sure about the demand for balloons, consider buying already inflated balloons from your local grocery store or florist shop. You probably won't be able to put a markup on them (at this point), but the option will make your customers happy and show the versatility of your business. Think carefully about your delivery method before advertising this feature. Balloons can be cumbersome, particularly if you have them on several packages to be delivered at the same time. With any new idea, always stop to think it through beginning to end, from preparation to packaging and delivery. When the demand for balloons increases, check out your local party store to purchase them without air or helium. In most cases, you can also purchase a small tank of air. This will allow you to start adding a markup to your balloons sales. This also adds the convenience of not having to go out every time someone requests a balloon with a gift. Party City (if there's one near you) carries a large selection of balloons, both helium and regular. They also carry air tanks. Check your yellow pages or online for other local stores that carry party goods. When you're ready for larger balloon orders, Burton & Burton is a great wholesale source. Minimums are relatively low. They carry almost any style, color, design, theme, or size that you might need. They also carry other gift items that coordinate with many of the balloons. See their information in the "Where to Find It" chapter under "Gift Packaging Sources."

Chapter 10

Professional Touches

INGREDIENT LABELS

It's informative, professional, and in some cases a requirement to attach a descriptive label or card to each package. Your customers will appreciate knowing more about the food they're eating. It's easy to create your own ingredient labels or cards using a computer and word-processing software. To make creating your labels easier and faster, Avery has templates that you can download from the Internet. Just go online to www.avery.com. (A template is a guide that keeps you within the borders of the label or card that you have selected to use.) If you don't have a computer or access to one, a business service company like Kinko's will create the labels for you. In some areas, the health department or department of agriculture often requires ingredient labels before a health permit is issued. If labels are required for your products, one of these departments will give you instructions on how to create them.

CUSTOM PACKAGE LABELS

Add a personalized touch to boxes, bags, baskets, and any items that you package by using custom-printed labels. As with business cards, you can personalize a label with your choice of information: your company name, specialty, address, phone number, and so forth. There are many companies that offer custom labels. There are also many colors, shapes, papers (foil or clear), and sizes to choose from. You're sure to find one that's perfect. See the "Where to Find It" chapter under "Put Your Stamp on It."

Here's a tip: if possible, choose packaging before you choose labels. If you need to buy labels first, go for something that will look great on several different colors, sizes, and shapes of packages. Having a label that's versatile will save on the budget.

CUSTOM RIBBONS

You can add color and personalization to a gift with custom-printed ribbons. There are many sizes, colors, and types of ribbon materials available. You can have slogans, logos, theme messages, and more printed on the ribbon. See the "Where to Find It" chapter under "Gift Packaging Sources."

HEAT SEALING

Using a heat sealer to seal cellophane bags will keep your baked goods and packaged snacks fresh and protected, and also gives the packages an upscale, professional look. Presentation plays a large part in making a sale.

CHAPTER 11

SET YOUR PRICES

It's impossible to know what percentage of your sales is profit if you don't know exactly how much it cost to produce or create the product. Before you can put a price on products, you must (a) determine exactly how much it cost to produce each item, (b) do a little market research, (c) decide if your products will be sold retail or wholesale, and (d) decide if your products will be sold on the local market, national market, or both. This process will take time. Approach it with patience, and follow the steps.

BREAK DOWN COSTS

Calculate the cost of all ingredients used in each product that you make. Ingredients as small as baking soda, baking powder, and salt will affect your bottom line. Don't forget cake boards, bakery boxes, and gift-packaging supplies. Also, when products are shipped to you, don't forget to calculate the total cost (shipping and handling plus product cost).

Next comes the difficult task of figuring out how much of your utility bills (electric, gas, and water) is work related. It's almost impossible to separate business use from personal use when you have a home-based business. So here's what I suggest: add at least 10 percent of the cost of ingredients to each product for utilities. For example, if the ingredients for a pound cake cost $5.00, 10 percent of that cost is $0.50, so you would add $0.50 to the price of each pound cake. This way you're not overlooking the cost of utilities and you're not overestimating it.

Last and very important is the cost of labor. Labor includes the time it takes to shop for items that are not shipped to you, ingredient preparation, the mixing and baking process, packaging finished products, and the time it takes to clean up the work area. So, how should you go about deciding labor cost? First, time the performance of each labor step mentioned above. Total the time for all steps. Break down the total time into hours or half hours, whichever works best for you. This will give you a labor time-frame for creating each product. If you have the capability of mixing and baking more than one product batch at a time, divide the total labor time by the number of batches. Next, decide how much your time and expertise is worth. Will it be $10.00, $15.00, $20.00, or more per hour? Finally, calculate the labor cost by multiplying the time it takes to make a product by the hourly rate you chose. For example: A pound cake takes an hour to make from start to finish. Multiply one hour times $15.00 (the hourly rate). Your labor cost for making a pound cake is $15.00.

These calculations will be time-consuming but extremely important to the health and survival of your business. I suggest you get a notebook or file folder and label it "Cost of Doing Business." As you calculate the cost of ounces, pieces, cups, teaspoons, dozens, pounds, etc., record these in your notebook or file. This information will also be helpful in the future when you create new recipes and need to know the cost of 4 eggs, 2 sticks of butter, 1 teaspoon of extract, etc. You'll find that this was time well spent.

CHECK MARKET PRICES

It's always good to be informed about what's going on in your trade or profession. Check the prices of bakeries, coffee shops, dessert shops, restaurants, Internet companies, and anyone in your area that sells a product comparable to yours. Sample their products when possible. Compare the quality, quantity, and cost of their products to yours. Do they offer discounts or promotions? If so, how much is the discount and how does the promotion program work? How are their products packaged? If they offer gift items, pay close attention to packaging and prices. Again, I suggest you create a folder to save the information you gather. Market comparisons are not done so that you can follow someone else's price structure. They are done to keep you well informed about your industry and to help you guard against underpricing or overpricing.

RETAIL OR WHOLESALE

Choosing to go retail is usually not a difficult decision, mainly because retail sales generate the full market value of your product and sometimes more. Brisk retail sales can put you on the fast track to reaching your goals and being successful. However, the downside to retail sales from a home-based business can be the lack of exposure to enough people who will buy at retail prices. Keep in mind that some business licenses restrict the number of vehicles allowed at your home at any given time. In other words, you're not allowed to turn your home into a retail store. Another unattractive feature of a retail sweets business is seasonality. The months for holidays and special occasions are November (Thanksgiving), December (Christmas), February (Valentine's Day), March or April (Easter), May (Mother's Day), and June (Father's Day). The other six months can be very unpredictable. If you decide to focus on retail only, plan a strong advertising campaign and don't forget to set aside sufficient advertising funds. Also, promote delivery options for customers instead of pickup options.

What about wholesale? Doing business with food-service companies such as restaurants, caterers, cafés, delis, grocery stores, and hotels can generate a steady income. In exchange for regular orders (at least once a week), these companies usually expect wholesale prices or deep discounts. Please understand, the retail price you get for a product will be quite different from what you get wholesale, unless, of course, your retail prices are unusually low. When a food-service company purchases products wholesale, they do so with the expectation of adding a markup to generate profit for their own business. If a cake retails for $30, the wholesale price might range from $15 to $20. You should also know that your products and prices will be compared with other wholesale products on the market. This is another reason for doing your market research. Food-service companies, like everyone else, want to get the most value for the dollars they spend. Here's a tip that might help to increase the size and dollar amount of your wholesale transactions: place product or dollar minimums on each order. For example, you could require wholesale customers to order at least six cakes or place an order of $100 or more.

Another consideration when working with wholesale accounts is charging for delivery. Sometimes food-service companies expect free delivery, depending on the amount of the order. To avoid any misunderstandings, add your delivery policy to the product information.

Wholesaling can be very rewarding and profitable. Just be careful not to take on more than you, your equipment, and your work space can handle. This mistake happens quite often with start-up small businesses. I'll share one of my early experiences with you. On one of my marketing days, I dropped off dessert samples to a restaurant. The owner liked them so much that he placed an order, on the spot, and asked if I could deliver them the next day. I was very excited and I needed the new account. So, I said yes. I rushed back home and made the desserts. In my excitement and haste to accept the order, I didn't consider something very important. The desserts he ordered needed to be chilled for a certain number of hours. Also, because it was the middle of summer in Georgia, I couldn't depend on weather temperatures to help keep the desserts cool in transit. Determined to follow through, I made the delivery as promised. When the boxes were opened, to check the desserts, the mousse cakes and tortes had fallen. They were all flat. Needless to say, I collected nothing for that delivery, and I lost the account. The point to this story is that things can go wrong even with small orders, particularly when there isn't sufficient time for preparation. Needs and desires sometimes overpower logic and clear thinking. You need the business, the money is music to your ears, the dollar signs register, and before you know it you've committed to something that you can't reasonably deliver.

Before you say yes to a small order, a large project, or an ongoing contract, take a realistic look at how much you can deliver and how often.

LOCAL OR NATIONAL SALES

The decision to do business locally or expand to other cities and states will be determined by your ability to manufacture and create products on demand and your ability to package those products for shipping and delivery. Packing and shipping can be a business in itself. It can be very time consuming. For more on packaging, delivery, and shipping see chapter 14. After a little research, you might decide that a mix of local and national sales would be great for your business.

CREATE YOUR PRICE FORMULAS

Most of us want to strike a happy medium with prices. We want our customers to feel that they are paying a fair price for the quality products and services we provide. At the same time, we need to be compensated for everything we invest from start to finish. After calculating, checking, and researching, it's time to create a formula for your prices. Ask yourself, am I OK with a minimal payoff for everything I invest? Or will I set prices to reflect my talent, expertise, great customer service and premium products? Don't give your time and knowledge away. You don't want to price yourself out of the market. At the same time, your prices should not be the lowest.

To further assist you with setting prices, I have listed three formulas used in my business for many years.

1. Stock and resell. When I purchase something that only needs to be stocked for resale, I usually add a 100 percent markup plus the cost of shipping and handling. These are usually items such as cheese straws, specialty pretzels, chips, and popcorn.

2. Buy and package for resale. When I purchase nuts, candies, and pretzels in bulk, these products need to be weighed, bagged, sealed, and labeled. To the cost of each unit of product, I usually add a 100 percent markup, plus another 100 percent markup on packaging (like cello bags and labels). I also add the cost of shipping and handling and $0.50 to $1.00 for labor, depending on the quantity of product in each package.

3. Making it from scratch. Products that I make myself can be the most difficult to price. Of course, I start with a 100 percent markup on all ingredients and packaging (like bakery boxes, boards, etc.), and I add 5 to 10 percent of the ingredients cost for utilities. Then we come to the big item, *labor.* Everyone has a different way of deciding labor cost. I usually factor in the amount of time it takes to make a product and the level of difficulty. Pound cakes, brownies, muffins, and cookies are relatively simple in construction. Layered, frosted cakes, by contrast, can be much more difficult and time consuming.

One of the best ways to decide labor cost is to walk yourself through the process of making the products. Start at the very beginning, which is usually prep (measuring ingredients). Continue step by step, not omitting the smallest details, and remember; labor is not over until your work area is completely cleaned up and the product is packaged and ready for delivery or pickup. This should give you a feel for the amount of labor and time required for each item.

Your price formula. After all of the research and calculations are done, the following formula can be used to set your prices: *cost of ingredients + cost of packaging + utilities + labor* will equal a fair market price for your products.

NEGOTIATING PRICES

I know very little about the how-tos of professional negotiating, but I have learned a few things from trial and error. When starting a new business, we are very excited about the mention or prospect of our first large order. Caught up in the excitement of getting a large order or contract, we sometimes give away more than is necessary to close the sale and make the customer happy. If you're discussing a large order, the potential customer may ask for a cut or discount off your regular price. What should you do? Don't rush to give a quote unless you've thought it through prior to the conversation. Simply explain that you need to get quotes from your vendors to see how much of a discount you will be able to offer. This will give you enough time to check quantity prices, negotiate with your suppliers, and come up with a well-thought-out proposal. If this is an in-town delivery, offer free delivery and a small discount (such as 5 percent) off the regular price instead of giving a large discount off the regular prices. Everyone loves a *free* offer, and the combination might sound like an even bigger deal. This idea will probably work best if you're making the delivery yourself or you have a company that offers reasonable rates on large deliveries. Also, it's a great idea to submit your quote or proposal in writing. This way, there's no confusion later about the details of the agreement.

CHAPTER 12

WHO WILL BUY YOUR PRODUCTS?

Family, friends, neighbors, coworkers, organizations, small businesses, corporate businesses, and more are potential customers. Almost everyone loves great homemade products. Consider the following:

Companies large and small send thank-you gifts to their customers and clients at holiday time, if at no other time of the year. Some law firms send thank-you gifts during the year for client referrals. There are many business-gift opportunities during the year, such as birthdays, anniversaries, sympathy, apologies, get-well wishes, thank-yous (for various reasons), Valentine's Day, Fourth of July, Thanksgiving, Christmas, and more. One order from a company can sometimes generate thousands of dollars in sales.

Organizations have huge parties and celebrations for the holidays. Don't wait until November to start your sales promotions. Introduce yourself and your product early in the year, and as the fall season approaches, send out reminders about upcoming events and what your company has to offer.

Caterers often don't have time for baking or don't have a person on staff with baking expertise. Many caterers purchase desserts and pastries from other companies. Consider scaling down some of your products to bite-size (appetizer) servings. Showing versatility can be an advantage. Also be prepared to negotiate a discount. Usually when a person or company buys something with the intent of reselling it, they are looking for a discount from the retail price.

Restaurants, Cafés, and Delicatessens are fantastic accounts if you are interested in increasing the quantity that you produce at a lower price per item (wholesale). I discovered early on that restaurants are very receptive to trying products from a new vendor, especially when the products are made from scratch and taste as good as they look.

Remember: consistent quality is very important in getting business and keeping it.

Chapter 13

Marketing and Advertising

BUSINESS CARDS

Always keep business cards with you. Give a few to everyone that you know: family, friends, coworkers, and business associates. Include a card with any product that you sell. Business cards are relatively inexpensive and a great way to get necessary contact information to potential customers. Full-color photo business cards are also available.

POSTCARDS

Basic white postcards with black or color ink can be used to announce your opening, a special sale, a new item, and much more. A full-color or photo postcard will add even more excitement to your announcement. If you have a photo of your work or something that you think will give your sales a boost, definitely try the photo postcard. Full-color postcards are relatively inexpensive and postage is the same as regular postcards. Sources for these cards are listed in the "Where to Find It" chapter under "Your Product in Pictures." Since most people don't take the time to open mail that appears to be advertising, your postcard will be noticed without any extra effort.

BROCHURES

If you have a computer and enjoy word processing, you can make your own brochures using basic colored paper or theme-design paper. If you're not interested in doing it yourself, most printing companies and business-service companies like Kinko's will do it for you. Shop two or three places for the best price, service, and product. If the budget allows, add a few photos of your product to the brochure. If you don't have photos, consider using a theme-design paper. These specialty papers can be found at major office-supply stores, paper warehouses, Kinko's and by special order. See the "Where to Find It" chapter under "Specialty Papers."

MAGNETIC SIGNS

If you have a car, truck, or van, this is a fantastic idea. You can attach magnetic signs to one or both sides of your vehicle. They can be easily removed when necessary. Best of all, everywhere your vehicle goes, someone will have the opportunity to see your ad and get information. Magnetic signs are usually available in three or more sizes. Most printing companies, including Kinko's, offer them. If you have a photo of your product, it can be included along with phone numbers and other information. Choose print that is large enough to be easily read. Avoid making the sign too busy. Too much information can be difficult to read if the car is not parked or standing still.

PROMOTIONAL ITEMS

T-shirts, aprons, caps, pens, key rings, calendars, and similar items can keep your name and number in front of thousands of people because of constant handling and use. These items also make nice thank-you gifts. Check the "Where to Find It" chapter under "Promotional and Advertising Items."

WEB SITE

The benefits of having a Web site can be enormous, but remember, you must advertise to generate traffic and attract shoppers to your Web site. If you decide in favor of an online store, also plan a strategy to bring in shoppers. Many companies offer Web site services ranging from "build it yourself" to "tell us what you want and we'll handle everything for you." If you hire a company to create a Web site, make sure they understand exactly what you have in mind or specifically what your needs are. If you're on a budget, be careful not to agree to costly, fancy features that won't serve your purposes. Do a little research. Check out online companies such as www.register.com. Compare rates and specials to other companies. If you have a membership with Sam's Club or Costco Wholesale, consider taking advantage of the Web site packages offered by these companies.

My Web site, www.uniqueoccasions.biz, is a "build-it-yourself" site purchased through Costco. As a totally inexperienced person in Web site building, I decided to test the waters. I wanted to see if it would be as easy as the Web company promised in its advertising. It was very time consuming, challenging, confusing, interesting, and fun. If you have more time than money and a little know-how, maybe this is the route for you. Don't forget, you'll still have to advertise your Web site. Otherwise, no one will know it's there. My Web site is up and functioning, but it still requires hours of updating as products and prices change. There are still many things that I don't know about building and maintaining a Web site. I'm learning as I go. Good luck with your online venture!

NETWORKING ASSOCIATIONS

These groups provide opportunities to make business contacts and advertise. The smaller the group, the more affordable the membership or participation fee. Look for a group that offers display tables, booths, or the opportunity to hand out samples. Check the yellow pages or the Internet for associations in your area.

BARTER AND TRADE ORGANIZATIONS

Bartering is a relatively inexpensive way to get your name out there and to enjoy a break from using cash to pay for everything. Most organizations have members from a variety of businesses, such as printing, travel, magazines, newspapers, photographers, plumbers, electricians, heating and air, construction, restaurants, caterers, and business services. Most organizations require a membership fee. Research the organization thoroughly before you make any commitments or pay fees. You need to know what types of businesses are members and if they offer anything that you need or want in trade. Don't forget to ask if you can set a limit or cutoff on the amount you trade in a certain period of time. If you're unclear about the smallest detail, don't be afraid to ask questions. You will be happier with the organization if you have a thorough understanding of what's involved and how things work. I credit a trade organization with introducing me to companies that have given me the biggest and most profitable accounts to date. The money spent for membership was a great payoff.

Here's another idea: consider creating your own bartering opportunities not connected to an organization. Sometimes small businesses that provide products or services to you will be interested in trading for some of your products. These could be companies that make your business cards and brochures, do your lawn service, and more. Keep track of all barter transactions for tax purposes. The IRS classifies goods that you receive in trade as income. Your tax preparer can explain and give you more information.

PRINT ADS IN NEWSPAPERS, MAGAZINES, AND OTHER MEDIA

This approach works better for some businesses than others. You should expect a slow response. According to statistics, ads must be published two or three times before they are noticed and maybe a few times more before someone is moved to make a purchase. Consult your budget before placing the first ad, and proceed with caution.

SALES AND ACCOUNT REPRESENTATIVES

At the start, this might sound a bit grand or costly for your small business, but it doesn't have to be. Consider hiring one or two people on a commission basis. Offer them a percentage of each sale that they generate. This can save you a lot of risky advertising, and you're paying out money *only* when you make money. Make sure your sales people have a thorough knowledge of your business and products. Don't forget to give them business cards and brochures or flyers with product information.

SAMPLES, SAMPLES, SAMPLES

Samples and word of mouth are probably your best and least expensive means of advertising. While pictures and descriptions are great, there's nothing like tasting the product. Your objective is to let everyone know that your baked goods taste as good or better than they look. Try sampling your products with organizations, schools, and businesses that gather for meetings and other functions. Community fairs are also great opportunities for exposure.

Here are a few more marketing tips:

1. Always include a business card with your product.
2. Even if you have a Web site, it's a good idea to include product information along with your business card. Some food-service companies, such as restaurants, require a list of ingredients for each product that you're sampling. This is not a bad idea, since promoting the quality ingredients that you use will give them another reason to do business with you.
3. If you're presenting product samples in a bakery box, make sure it's clean, free of grease spots, and is the appropriate size, so that the samples won't arrive damaged. The box should also be properly sealed to ensure product safety and freshness.
4. Dress appropriately for sales and marketing appointments. You're a professional business person. You and your home-based business should be taken just as seriously as the person who owns a store in

the mall or a shopping center.

5. When planning marketing appointments, remember, you don't get a second chance to make a first impression. Take advantage of each opportunity and make the most of it. HAPPY MARKETING!

CHAPTER 14

DELIVERY AND SHIPPING

Most freshly baked products are highly perishable. They need to be protected from extreme temperatures, lengthy shipping, and possible mishandling. The type of product that you make, the distance that it has to travel, the urgency to receive it, and your customer's ability to pay will determine the best method of delivery. Remember, presentation is very important. If you're not sure that your product will arrive in good condition, don't ship it. If baked goods are expected for a special occasion and they arrive damaged, you might lose the customer. The situation will be worsened if there's not enough time to prepare and ship more. The following is a list of the most popular or frequently used delivery systems.

DO IT YOURSELF

A do-it-yourself delivery system can range anywhere from making the deliveries yourself or having friends and family deliver for you, to hiring someone to make deliveries using your personal vehicle (not the best idea) or your company vehicle. Most small businesses start with do-it-yourself deliveries; but as business increases, owners may be unable to work long hours at the shop and also make deliveries. Family and friends are not always available to help. So you're faced with making a decision about how you will get product to your customers safely, affordably, and in a timely fashion. If you're considering buying a company vehicle and hiring a driver, thoroughly research and consider what you can budget for the monthly vehicle payment, insurance, payroll, gas, regular vehicle maintenance, and the total delivery area to be covered. I speak from experience when I say that delivery is very time consuming, and it's almost a business in itself. Sometimes it's best to turn delivery over to an outside source.

COURIER SERVICE

Couriers are great for local deliveries but can be expensive. However, for many years I've provided my customers with fresh-baked products and gourmet gifts by way of courier. A combination of affordable rates, saved time, and convenience makes this the best choice for me. Currently, I use two courier companies that offer different services, plans, and prices. I'm fortunate to have one company very close to my business. They offer next-day service, which means they will pick up packages from me today and deliver them tomorrow to any place in the state of Georgia for a minimum of $8.50. This fee covers a delivery of ten pounds or less to one address. Deliveries are guaranteed to arrive by 5:00 PM. The other courier delivers only to the Atlanta metropolitan area. They are a fairly large company and have the ability to handle large deliveries. They offer four different plans ranging from delivery within thirty minutes of pickup to same-day delivery before 5:00 PM. If you're interested in using a courier service but you're not sure if it's the best option for you, do some research. Call the companies in your area. Ask if they have information that they can send to you. Ask about their range of delivery, whether they offer same-day delivery, next-day delivery, or both. Ask if you are in their free pick-up zone. Compare services and prices. If your business is located in the Atlanta area and you would like to contact my courier companies, their information is as follows: Mid Georgia Courier (next-day service) at 770-991-1084, and CourierSouth (same-day service for small and large deliveries) at 770-246-0007.

UPS

This is my favorite out-of-town delivery company and probably the most widely used carrier for ground service. You have the convenience of pick-up service for a fee. UPS also offers business discounts. Check the Web site (www.

ups.com) or call customer service 1-800-742-5877 for more information.

FEDEX

Again, you have the convenience of pick-up service for a fee. FedEx also offers business discounts. Check the Web site (www.fedex.com) or call customer service at 1-800-463-3339 for more information.

DHL

Check the Web site (www.dhl-usa.com) or call customer service at 1-800-225-5345.

HOW TO PACKAGE ITEMS FOR SHIPPING

Before handing over your products to *any* delivery or shipping company, make sure that the products are properly packaged for weather conditions, distance of travel, and mode of travel. Most shipping companies deliver thousands of packages a day. They're probably not going to be gentle with your packages even when they're labeled as fragile. To assist you with making packaging and shipping decisions, consider the following:

Frosted cakes are very fragile, highly perishable, and don't travel well unless frozen. Melted or runny frosting will not make a good impression. Likewise, soft, soupy cheesecakes don't impress. Most companies that ship frosted cakes or cheesecakes (out of their area) freeze them first, then pack and ship in special thick-wall Styrofoam containers. You can also use ice packs or dry ice if the thick-wall Styrofoam containers are too costly or not available. When shipping frozen products, make sure the customer understands that the product(s) might arrive frozen and why. This information should be provided to the customer as a "need-to-know" and a courtesy. See the "Where to Find It" chapter under "Packing and Shipping Supplies."

Pound cakes are relatively easy to pack and ship, and they travel well no matter the weather. If you're looking for a container to protect the cakes and keep them fresh, try tins. Just wrap the cake with restaurant-quality plastic wrap, or place it in a large cello bag (food approved), and place it in the tin. Bertels Can Company makes a five-pound tin especially for pound cakes. They carry a dozen or more designs along with heat-seal bands and shipping boxes made especially for the tins. It's the perfect packaging with one-stop shopping. See the "Where to Find It" chapter under "Gift Packaging Sources."

Cookies, brownies, and similar products are not difficult to pack and ship, but they require close attention to inside packaging to avoid breaking and crumbling. They can be hand delivered by courier or shipped across country. Weather conditions are not a factor as long as they are packaged properly. See the "Where to Find It" chapter under "Packing and Shipping Supplies" for companies that carry many sizes of shipping boxes and all of the necessary packaging supplies. Always pack with care. It will assist greatly in a safe arrival.

Here are a few tips that might assist you with research and setting shipping prices:

- Call the leading shipping companies and ask for quotes.
- Do some research. Find out what other companies with similar products charge and compare their prices to the quotes you received.
- Pay close attention to other companies' shipping rules (when the order has to be placed to receive it by a certain date). You can pick up helpful tips from the pros and profit from their expertise.
- If you're shipping perishable products, make sure they're scheduled to arrive before the weekend. It's not a good idea for fresh baked products to spend the weekend in a warehouse.
- Don't forget to factor in the cost of packaging materials (boxes, tape, labels, Styrofoam, etc.).
- Make the most of your shipping dollars. Always use boxes that are the proper size for the product(s) you're shipping. Shipping companies generally charge by the size of package as well as weight. If the box is too large for the contents, you'll be paying for *unused* space.

- If you're unsure about how well your products will ship, try sending something across country as a test. Let the recipient know that the shipment is a test and that you will need accurate and honest feedback.

- Call the delivery carriers, or go to their Web sites, to get packing and shipping requirements. Many things have changed in the past few years. New rules and requirements can affect your labor, time, and budget.

Chapter 15

Recipes

This chapter includes some of my favorite recipes. A few of them have been used in my business and others for personal events and special occasions. This chapter is not intended to provide you with all of the recipes that you might need to start a business. I chose these recipes because most of them are basic, relatively easy, and adaptable. If you don't have recipes of your own, these recipes will give you a good foundation or starting point. And by changing a few ingredients, you can create a different product. Keep in mind, *your* recipes and products should reflect *your* personality, *your* potential market, and the vision that you have for *your* business. Don't be afraid to make changes and experiment. *Have fun!*

EASY FUDGE BROWNIES

This recipe could be the perfect start to a great brownie business. They're quick and relatively simple to make. The pure butter, chocolate, and vanilla extract give them a real homemade taste.

4 ounces unsweetened chocolate
¾ cup (1 ½ sticks) butter
2 cups sugar
3 large eggs
1 teaspoon pure vanilla extract
1 cup all-purpose flour
1 cup coarsely chopped pecans or walnuts (optional)
13 × 9 inch baking pan
PAM cooking spray or equivalent

1. Position a rack in the center of the oven and preheat to 350°.

2. Microwave unsweetened chocolate and butter in large microwaveable bowl on high for 2 minutes or until butter is melted. Stir until chocolate is completely melted.

3. Stir in sugar. Add eggs and vanilla. Mix well, but *do not beat.* Add flour and pecans. Stir until well blended. Spread into baking pan sprayed with PAM.

4. Bake 30 to 35 minutes or until toothpick inserted in center comes out with fudgy crumbs. Do not over bake. Cool brownies completely. Cut into desired sizes. Recipe yields 12 to 24 servings.

Brownies can be glazed, but think first of how you're going to package them for delivery. A glaze can melt and become sticky in warm weather. Brownies that are sticking together when the package is opened will not make a good presentation. If you decide to glaze them, here's a quick recipe: melt 2 ounces of semi-sweet baking chocolate, and drizzle each square with melted chocolate.

Marbled Cream Cheese Brownies

A generous cream cheese mixture is swirled through these fudgy brownies!
They make unforgettable gifts at holiday time and throughout the year.

6 ounces semisweet chocolate, coarsely chopped

3 ounces unsweetened chocolate, coarsely chopped

16 ounces cream cheese, softened

2 cups granulated sugar, divided

4 large eggs, at room temperature

1 tablespoon pure vanilla extract, divided

1 cup (2 sticks) butter, softened

1 cup all-purpose flour

¼ teaspoon salt

13 × 9 inch baking pan

PAM cooking spray or equivalent

1. Position a rack in the center of the oven and preheat to 350°.

2. In the top of a double boiler over hot, not simmering, water, melt the chocolates, stirring often until smooth. Chocolates can also be melted in a microwave. Remove the top part of the double boiler from the bottom and cool the chocolate until tepid.

3. In a large bowl, using an electric mixer set a medium speed, beat together the cream cheese and 1/3 cup of the sugar until smooth. Beat in one of the eggs and 1 teaspoon of the vanilla until combined.

4. In another large bowl, using an electric mixer set at medium speed, beat the butter and remaining 1 2/3 cups of sugar until combined. Beat in the remaining 3 eggs, one at a time, beating well after each addition. Beat in the melted chocolate and the remaining 2 teaspoons of vanilla extract. On low speed, mix in the flour and salt, just until combined.

5. Spray the baking pan. Scrape all but 1 cup of the chocolate batter into the pan and smooth the top with a rubber spatula. Spread the cream cheese mixture evenly over the batter. Spoon the reserved chocolate batter over the cream cheese mixture. Pull a table knife or a small metal cake spatula

through the layers of batter in a zigzag fashion to create a marbled effect. Bake 33 to 38 minutes, or until a cake tester or toothpick inserted 2 inches from the center comes out slightly moist.

6. Cool completely. Cut into bars. Brownies can be refrigerated for several days provided they are covered or wrapped properly. Recipe yields 24 to 36 bars.

Ultimate Chocolate Chip Cookies

You can satisfy many tastes at once with these yummy treats.

2 ½ cups all-purpose flour
1 teaspoon baking soda
½ teaspoon salt
1 cup butter, softened
1 cup packed light brown sugar
¾ cup granulated sugar
2 large eggs
1 tablespoon vanilla
1 cup semisweet chocolate chips
1 cup milk chocolate chips
1 cup vanilla milk chips (white chocolate chips)
½ cup coarsely chopped pecans or walnuts

1. Preheat oven to 375°.

2. Combine flour, baking soda, and salt in medium bowl. Set aside.

3. Beat butter, brown sugar, and granulated sugar in large bowl until light and fluffy (using paddle beater). Beat in eggs and vanilla. Add flour mixture to butter mixture; mix on low speed until well blended. Stir in chips and pecans.

4. Measure dough with a cookie scoop (for size consistency) and place evenly on parchment-lined or ungreased cookie sheets. Bake 10 to 12 minutes or until edges are golden brown. Let cookies stand on cookie sheets until completely cool to prevent breaking. Recipe yields 4 to 6 dozen cookies, depending on scoop size.

If you don't like all three flavors of chips, you can use 3 cups of one flavor or a mix of two flavors. Be adventurous. Don't be afraid to make changes.

CHUNKY PEANUT BUTTER COOKIES

These chewy, homemade cookies have the perfect blend of butter and peanut butter.

1 cup butter (2 sticks), softened
1 cup chunky peanut butter
1 cup granulated sugar
1 cup brown sugar
2 eggs
1 teaspoon vanilla extract
2 ½ cups all-purpose flour
1 ½ teaspoons baking soda
¼ teaspoon salt

1. Preheat oven to 375°.

2. Thoroughly cream butter, peanut butter, sugars, eggs, and vanilla. Sift together dry ingredients; blend into creamed mixture.

3. Measure dough with a cookie scoop and place on parchment-lined or ungreased cookie sheets. Bake 10 to 12 minutes. Cool completely. Recipe yields 4 to 6 dozen cookies, depending on the scoop size. Creamy peanut butter can be substituted for the chunky style.

For a variation, add 1 cup of semisweet chocolate chips after adding dry ingredients.

Oatmeal Raisin Cookies

Butter, cinnamon, and nutmeg make these yummy cookies stand out from the rest.

1 cup butter (2 sticks), softened
¾ cup granulated sugar
1 ¼ cup firmly packed brown sugar
2 large eggs
1 teaspoon vanilla extract
2 cups all-purpose flour
1 ½ teaspoon baking soda
½ teaspoon salt
1 ½ teaspoons cinnamon
½ teaspoon ground nutmeg
1 ½ cups quick-cooking oats, uncooked
1 cup raisins
1 ½ cups chopped pecans or walnuts

1. Preheat oven to 375°.

2. Beat butter at medium speed with an electric mixer until creamy; gradually add sugars, beating well. Add eggs and vanilla; beat well.

3. Combine flour and next 4 ingredients; gradually add to butter mixture; mix until well blended. Stir in oats, raisins, and nuts.

4. Measure dough with a cookie scoop and place on parchment-lined or ungreased cookie sheets. Bake 8 to 10 minutes until lightly browned. Cool completely. Recipe yields 5 to 7 dozen cookies, depending on scoop size.

Oatmeal Chocolate Chip Cookies

Omit the cinnamon and nutmeg from recipe above. Stir 2 cups (12 ounces) semisweet chocolate morsels and 3 grated bars (1.5 ounce) milk chocolate into cookie dough before baking.

WHITE CHOCOLATE MACADAMIA NUT COOKIES

Pure butter and the hint of coconut flavoring make these cookies unforgettable.

½ cup butter, softened
½ cup shortening
¾ cup firmly packed brown sugar
½ cup sugar
1 large egg
1 teaspoon vanilla extract
¼ teaspoon coconut flavoring
2 cups all-purpose flour
1 teaspoon baking soda
½ teaspoon salt
6 ounces white chocolate chips or chunks
1 cup macadamia nuts or pecans, chopped

1. Preheat oven to 375°.

2. Beat butter and shortening at medium speed with an electric mixer until creamy; gradually add sugars, beating well. Add egg vanilla extract and coconut flavoring; beat well. Combine flour, baking soda, and salt; gradually add to butter mixture, beating well. Stir in white chocolate and nuts.

3. Measure dough with a cookie scoop and place on parchment-lined or ungreased cookie sheets.

4. Bake 8 to 10 minutes or until lightly browned. Cool completely. Recipe yields 4 to 5 dozen, depending on scoop size.

Best Butter Cookies

This recipe is very adaptable to many different flavors and personalities. I've added a few variations at the end of the recipe.

1 cup butter, softened
1 cup sugar
2 large egg yolks
¾ teaspoon vanilla extract
½ teaspoon almond extract
½ teaspoon lemon extract
2 cups all-purpose flour
1 teaspoon baking powder
¼ teaspoon salt

1. Preheat oven to 375°.

2. Combine flour, baking powder, and salt. Set aside.

3. Cream butter; gradually add sugar, beating until well blended. Add egg yolks, one at a time, beating well after each addition. Stir in flavorings. Add flour mixture to butter mixture; mix well.

4. Measure dough with cookie scoop and place on parchment-lined or ungreased cookie sheets. Bake 10 to 12 minutes or until lightly browned. Cool completely before removing from pan. Recipe yields 3 to 4 dozen, depending on scoop size.

Variations:

Butter Pecan Cookies: Add 1 cup chopped pecans after adding flour mixture, or press a pecan half into the center of each cookie scoop after placing it on the baking sheet.

Southern Lemon Tea Cookies: Omit vanilla and almond extracts. Add 2 teaspoons freshly squeezed lemon juice and 1 tablespoon of lemon zest (grated lemon rind).

Tip: Get double-duty from the lemons by removing the zest before squeezing the juice. When zesting or grating lemon rind, be careful to remove only the yellow skin and not the white pith beneath, as this tends to be very bitter.

OLD-FASHIONED POUND CAKE

The pinch of nutmeg adds something special to the taste of this homemade cake.

2 cups butter, softened
2¾ cups sugar
6 large eggs
3¾ cups all-purpose flour
½ teaspoon salt
¼ teaspoon ground nutmeg
½ cup milk
1 teaspoon vanilla extract

1. Preheat oven to 325°.

2. Using a heavy stand mixer, beat butter at medium speed for 2 minutes or until creamy. Gradually add sugar, beating 5 to 7 minutes. Add eggs, one at a time, beating until yellow disappears.

3. Combine flour, salt, and nutmeg; add to butter mixture, alternating with the milk, beginning and ending with flour mixture. Mix at low speed after each addition just until mixture is blended. Stir in vanilla.

4. Spoon batter into a greased and floured 10-inch tube pan. Time saver: spray pan with PAM. Bake about 1 1/4 hours or until a wooden pick inserted in center comes out clean. Cool in pan for 20 to 25 minutes; remove from pan. Recipe yields 14 to 16 servings.

CHOCOLATE POUND CAKE

Coffee heightens and intensifies the chocolate taste in this moist dessert.

1 cup butter, softened

1 ½ cups sugar

4 large eggs

6 milk chocolate candy bars (1.5 ounce), melted (Hershey's suggested)

3 cups all-purpose flour

¼ teaspoon baking soda

1/8 teaspoon salt

1 cup buttermilk

1 tablespoon instant coffee granules (dissolved in buttermilk)

1 cup chopped pecans

½ cup chocolate syrup (Hershey's suggested)

2 teaspoons vanilla extract

powdered sugar (optional garnish)

1. Preheat oven to 325°.

2. Beat butter at medium speed with electric mixer for 2 minutes or until creamy. Gradually add sugar, beating 5 to 7 minutes. Add eggs, one at a time, beating after each addition just until yellow disappears. Add melted candy bars, stirring well.

3. Combine flour, baking soda, and salt; add to butter mixture, alternating with the buttermilk, beginning and ending with flour mixture. Mix at low speed after each addition just until blended. Stir in pecans, chocolate syrup, and vanilla.

4. Pour batter into a greased and floured 10-inch tube pan. Time saver: spray pan with PAM. Bake about 1 hour and 5 minutes or until a wooden pick inserted in center comes out clean. Cool in pan 20 to 25 minutes; remove from pan and cool completely. For a decorative touch, sprinkle with powdered sugar. Recipe yields 14 to 16 servings.

Coconut Cream Cheese Pound Cake

This is a perfect all-year pound cake. It ships and stores well.

½ cup butter, softened
½ cup shortening
1 package cream cheese (8 ounces), softened
3 cups sugar
6 large eggs
3 cups all-purpose flour
¼ teaspoon baking soda
¼ teaspoon salt
1 package frozen flake grated coconut, thawed (6 ounces, equals 1 ¾ cups)
1 teaspoon vanilla extract
½ teaspoon coconut flavoring

1. Preheat oven to 325°.

2. Beat butter, shortening, and cream cheese at medium speed with an electric mixer for 2 minutes until creamy. Gradually add sugar, beating 5 to 7 minutes. Add eggs, one at a time, beating after each addition just until yellow disappears.

3. Combine flour, baking soda, and salt; add to butter mixture, beating at low speed just until blended. Stir in coconut, vanilla, and coconut flavoring.

4. Pour batter into a greased and floured 10-inch tube pan. Time saver: spray pan with PAM. Bake about 1 1/4 hours or until wooden pick inserted in center comes out clean. Cool in pan 20 to 25 minutes; remove from pan and cool completely. Recipe yields 14 to 16 servings.

SOUR CREAM CINNAMON POUND CAKE

Consider packaging this yummy cake as a gift along with gourmet coffee or herbal tea. It's irresistible.

4½ teaspoons sugar

3 teaspoons cinnamon

1 cup butter, softened

2 cups sugar

2 large eggs

8 ounces sour cream

1 teaspoon vanilla extract

2 cups all-purpose flour, unsifted

1 teaspoon baking soda

¼ teaspoon salt

1 cup finely chopped pecans

1. Preheat oven to 325°.

2. Combine sugar and cinnamon. Set aside.

3. Cream butter and sugar. Add eggs, one at a time, beating until the yellow disappears.

4. Beat in sour cream and vanilla.

5. Mix together flour, baking soda, and salt. Slowly add to batter, mixing well.

6. Stir in pecans.

7. Pour 1/3 of the batter into a well-greased and floured 10-inch tube pan. Sprinkle batter with 1/3 of the sugar and cinnamon mixture. Pour 1/3 more of the batter and sprinkle with cinnamon and sugar. Pour in remaining batter and sprinkle with remaining cinnamon and sugar.

8. Bake 1 hour and 5 or10 minutes or until done. Recipe yields 14 to 16 servings.

CREAM CHEESE POUND CAKE

This cake is rich, moist, and special enough for a wedding cake creation.

1½ cups butter, softened
1 (8-ounce) package cream cheese, softened
3 cups sugar
6 large eggs
1 tablespoon vanilla extract
3 cups all-purpose flour
¼ teaspoon salt

1. Preheat oven to 300°.

2. Beat butter and cream cheese at medium speed with an electric mixer for 2 minutes or until mixture is creamy. Gradually add sugar, beating 5 to 7 minutes. Add eggs, one at a time, beating just until yellow disappears. Add vanilla, mix well.

3. Combine flour and salt; gradually add to butter mixture, beating at low speed after each addition just until blended. Pour batter into a greased and floured 10-inch tube pan. Time saver: spray pan with PAM.

4. Bake 1 hour and 30 minutes or until a wooden pick inserted in center of cake comes out clean. Cool in pan 20 to 25 minutes; remove from pan and cool completely. Recipe yields 14 to 16 servings.

LEMON CREAM CHEESE POUND CAKE

If you like the Cream Cheese Pound Cake above, try this lemony twist on that recipe.

Prepare cake as above with these changes:

Reduce vanilla extract to 1 teaspoon.

Add 2 teaspoons freshly squeezed lemon juice, 1 teaspoon lemon extract, and 2 teaspoons freshly grated lemon rind. Drizzle with Lemon Glaze (see "Frostings and Glazes").

Tip: Get double-duty from the lemons by removing the zest before squeezing the juice. When zesting or grating lemon rind, be careful to remove only the yellow skin and not the white pith beneath, as this tends to be very bitter.

SOUTHERN LEMON POUND CAKE

This is my Grandmother Hattie's recipe with a few special touches of my own.

1½ cups butter, softened

3 cups sugar

8 large eggs

1 teaspoon lemon extract

1 tablespoon grated lemon zest (rind)

2 tablespoons fresh-squeezed lemon juice

3 cups all-purpose flour

¼ teaspoon salt

1 recipe Lemon Glaze (see "Frostings and Glazes")

1. Preheat oven to 325°.

2. Beat butter and sugar at medium speed with an electric mixer for about 5 to 7 minutes. Add eggs, one at a time, beating after each addition just until yellow disappears.

3. Add lemon extract, lemon zest, and lemon juice. Beat until well blended.

3. Combine flour and salt; add to butter mixture, beating at low speed just until blended.

4. Pour batter into a greased and floured 10-inch tube pan. Time saver: spray pan with PAM. Bake about 1 hour and 25 minutes or until wooden pick inserted in center comes out clean. Cool in pan 20 to 25 minutes; remove from pan and cool completely. Drizzle with lemon glaze if desired. Recipe yields 14 to 16 servings.

Tip: Get double-duty from the lemons by removing the zest before squeezing the juice. When zesting or grating lemon rind, be careful to remove only the yellow skin and not the white pith beneath, as this tends to be very bitter.

YELLOW BUTTER CAKE

This basic recipe is quite versatile. It marries well with citrus flavorings, fruit fillings, fresh fruit, chocolate, and more.

1 cup butter, softened
2 cups sugar
4 large eggs
1½ teaspoons vanilla extract
3 cups flour
2 teaspoons baking powder
¼ teaspoon salt
1 cup milk

1. Preheat oven to 350°.

2. Beat butter and sugar at high speed with an electric mixer for about 3 to 5 minutes. Add eggs, one at a time, beating after each addition just until yellow disappears. Add vanilla and mix until well blended.

3. Sift together flour, baking powder, and salt; add to butter mixture, alternating with the milk, beginning and ending with flour mixture.

4. Grease and flour (or spray with PAM) three 9-inch pans or three 10-inch pans, depending on the thickness you would like the layers. Pour batter into pans.

5. Bake 20 to 25 minutes or until wooden pick inserted into center of cake comes out clean. Cool in pans 15 to 20 minutes; remove from pans and cool completely before filling or frosting. Tip: chilled layers handle much easier when frosting or filling. A 9-inch cake yields 12 to 14 servings and a 10-inch cake yields 14 to 18 servings.

Fresh Strawberry Torte

This is the ultimate fresh summer dessert. See photo on the cover.

3 pints fresh strawberries (washed, stems cut, and sliced) for 9-inch layers, 4 pints for 10-inch layers

3 layers Yellow Butter Cake

1 recipe Butter Cream Cheese Frosting (see "Frostings and Glazes")

1. Separate strawberry slices; save largest slices for top of cake.

2. Spread first cake layer with frosting; then arrange a generous amount of strawberry slices on top. Repeat with another layer of frosting and strawberries. Add third cake layer and repeat with frosting and strawberries. Refrigerate cake to avoid melted frosting or sliding layers. Remove from refrigerator 30 to 40 minutes prior to serving.

FABULOUS COCONUT CAKE

The coconut milk and cream cheese frosting add an extra special taste.

Bake the Yellow Butter Cake using ½ cup milk and ½ cup coconut milk.
1 14-ounce bag Baker's Coconut (avoid substitutions;
      other brands of coconut tend to be dry)
1 recipe Butter Cream Cheese Frosting (see "Frostings and Glazes")

1. Spread first layer with frosting and sprinkle with a generous amount of coconut. Repeat with second layer.

2. Add third cake layer; frost sides and top of cake. Sprinkle generous amount of coconut around sides and on top of cake. For a decorative touch, garnish cake on top with cherries, pineapple, candied lemon, or orange slices. You can also garnish with piped frosting.

GRANDMA'S CHOCOLATE CAKE

In some areas of the South, a yellow butter cake covered with a rich chocolate frosting is referred to as chocolate cake. When I was a child, my grandmother made a chocolate cake, very much like this one, at least three Sundays of the month. It was a treat. I made a few changes to her butter cake recipe and added my creamy fudge frosting. If you're looking for a great product that will grab everyone's attention, consider this made-from-scratch, six-layer chocolate cake. It's impressive, elegant, and appetizing. You could build a business and become known from baking just this one cake.

*Make 4 or 6 layers of Yellow Butter Cake.
1 recipe Chocolate Fudge Frosting (see "Frostings and Glazes")

1. Spread frosting on first layer; top with second cake layer and frost. Repeat with remaining layers.

2. Frost sides and top of cake. For decorative touches, sprinkle top of cake with nuts, chocolate shavings, or miniature chocolate chips. You can also garnish with piped frosting.

*An easy way to make 6 layers is to bake 3 layers; cut each of the 3 layers in half horizontally, creating two layers from each single layer. Chill layers first for easier cutting, handling, and frosting.

TRIPLE-LAYER LEMON CAKE

This is the perfect spring-and-summer dessert. It's creamy, buttery, sweet, and a bit tangy. It could be a signature dessert for your company.

2 1/3 cups all-purpose flour
1½ teaspoons baking powder
½ teaspoon baking soda
¼ teaspoon salt
1 cup butter, softened
2 cups sugar
2 teaspoons finely grated lemon peel
2 tablespoons lemon juice
4 eggs
1 cup buttermilk
1 recipe Lemon Curd (see "Frostings and Glazes")
1 recipe Lemon Cream Cheese Frosting (see "Frostings and Glazes")

1. Preheat oven to 350°.
2. Grease and lightly flour (or spray with PAM) three 9-inch pans.
3. Combine flour, baking powder, baking soda, and salt; set aside.
4. Beat butter with an electric mixer on high speed for 30 seconds. Add sugar, lemon peel, and lemon juice; beat until well combined. Add eggs, one at a time, beating until the yellow disappears. Add flour mixture, alternating with the buttermilk, beating on low speed after each addition just until combined. Pour into prepared pans.
5. Bake 25 to 30 minutes or until a wooden toothpick inserted near the center of each cake layer comes out clean. Cool cakes in pans.
6. To assemble, place a cake layer on a cake plate or board. Spread with half of the Lemon Curd. Top with second layer; spread with remaining Lemon Curd. Top with third layer. Frost top and sides with Lemon Cream Cheese Frosting. Cover and store cake in the refrigerator for up to 3 days. Let stand at room temperature for 30 to 45 minutes before serving. For a decorative touch, garnish with lemon peel curls. Recipe yields 12 to 14 Servings.

Best-Ever Carrot Cake

Positively unforgettable!
This is a very moist cake with perfect spices and the ultimate frosting.

2 cups all-purpose flour, sifted
2 teaspoons baking powder
1½ teaspoons baking soda
1½ teaspoons salt
1½ teaspoons ground cinnamon
½ teaspoon nutmeg
2 cups sugar
1½ cups vegetable oil
¼ cup buttermilk
4 large eggs
1 teaspoon vanilla extract
*2 cups finely shredded carrots
8½ ounces crushed pineapple, drained
¾ cup chopped pecans
¾ cup flaked coconut
¾ cup raisins (optional)
1 recipe Buttermilk Glaze (see "Frostings and Glazes")
1 recipe Cream Cheese Frosting (see "Frostings and Glazes")

1. Preheat oven to 350°.

2. Grease and lightly flour (or spray with PAM) three 9-inch pans.

3. In large mixing bowl, sift together flour, baking powder, baking soda, salt, cinnamon, and nutmeg. Add sugar, oil, buttermilk, eggs, and vanilla. Beat in electric mixer at medium speed for 1 minute. Stir in carrots, pineapple, pecans, coconut, and raisins. Pour into prepared pans.

4. Bake 30 to 35 minutes or until done. Brush Buttermilk Glaze over layers. Cool in pans completely. Frost with Cream Cheese Frosting. Recipe yields 12 to 14 servings.

*Carrots must be finely shredded or they may sink to the bottom of the pan during baking.

ITALIAN CREAM CAKE

This cake is always a favorite. It's perfect for many occasions, especially weddings and holidays.

1 cup butter, softened
½ cup shortening
2 cups sugar
2 cups sifted flour
1 teaspoon baking soda
1 cup buttermilk
4 large egg yolks
1 teaspoon vanilla extract
1 cup chopped pecans or walnuts
1 cup coconut
4 stiffly beaten large egg whites
1 recipe Cream Cheese Frosting (see "Frostings and Glazes")

1. Preheat oven to 350°.

2. Grease and lightly flour (or spray with PAM) three 9-inch pans.

3. Cream butter, shortening, and sugar until light and fluffy, about 3 to 4 minutes. Add flour, buttermilk, soda, egg yolks, vanilla, nuts, and coconut. Fold in egg whites. Pour into prepared pans.

4. Bake in prepared pans for 25 minutes or until done. Cool completely in pans. Frost and stack layers. Frost sides and top of cake. For a decorative touch, sprinkle top of cake with coconut and nuts. Recipe yields 12 to 14 servings.

FROSTINGS AND GLAZES

CREAM CHEESE FROSTING

1 8-ounce package cream cheese, softened
½ cup butter, softened
1 pound powdered sugar
2 teaspoons pure vanilla extract

Beat cream cheese, butter, and vanilla with an electric mixer until light and fluffy. Gradually add powdered sugar, beating well after each addition. Beat until light and fluffy. *Do not overbeat.* If you've never made this frosting, it could take a couple of times to get the timing and consistency just right. It's really easy and one of the best frostings ever.

LEMON CREAM CHEESE FROSTING

1 teaspoon lemon peel, finely grated
1 teaspoon lemon juice
1 8-ounce package cream cheese, softened
½ cup butter, softened
4½ to 4¾ cups powdered sugar, sifted

In a medium mixing bowl combine cream cheese, butter, and lemon juice; beat with electric mixer on low to medium speed until light and fluffy. Gradually add 2 cups sugar, beating well. Gradually beat in 2½ to 2¾ cups additional sugar to make frosting that is easy to spread. Stir in the lemon peel.

EASY CHOCOLATE FUDGE FROSTING

8 ounces semisweet baking chocolate

½ cup butter

1 16-ounce package powdered sugar

1/3 cup milk

2 teaspoons vanilla extract

Microwave chocolate and butter in large microwaveable bowl on high for 2 minutes. Stir until chocolate is completely melted. Add powdered sugar and vanilla extract. Beat with electric mixer on low speed until well blended. Gradually add milk, beating until well blended. Beat on high speed until smooth and creamy.

LEMON CURD

½ cup sugar

2 teaspoons cornstarch

2 teaspoons finely shredded lemon peel

¼ cup freshly squeezed lemon juice

¼ cup butter

2 beaten eggs

In saucepan combine sugar and cornstarch. Stir in lemon peel and juice. Add butter. Cook and stir until thickened and bubbly. Stir half of lemon mixture into eggs. Pour egg mixture into the pan. Cook and stir 2 minutes more. Cover with waxed paper; cool.

Buttermilk Glaze

½ cup sugar
¼ cup buttermilk
¼ cup butter
2 teaspoons light corn syrup
½ teaspoon vanilla

In a medium saucepan combine sugar, buttermilk, butter, and corn syrup. Bring to a boil; reduce heat. Cook and stir for 4 minutes. Remove saucepan from heat and stir in vanilla. Brush glaze evenly over warm cake layers. Try this glaze over other breads and cakes, such as zucchini bread, banana nut bread, apple cake, fruit cake, and more. It adds moisture and preserves freshness for several days.

Lemon Glaze

1 cup powdered sugar
¼ teaspoon lemon extract
1 teaspoon grated lemon peel
2 to 3 tablespoons freshly squeezed lemon juice

In medium size bowl, combine powdered sugar, lemon extract, lemon peel, and lemon juice. Mix until smooth. If you like a little color in your glaze, add yellow food color by sticking a toothpick in the color then stirring it into the glaze with the toothpick. Take the little-at-a-time approach until you have the desired color.

CHAPTER 16

BAKING TIPS

There are hundreds of how-tos, dos, and don'ts, far too many to cover in this book. However, I did feel it necessary to discuss a few basics. These tips will, I hope, get you off to a great start and continue to assist you along the way. You can find more great tips and general baking information in recipe books by *Southern Living, Better Homes and Gardens,* Hershey's publications, and more. Spend a few dollars from time to time on good resource books. It's an *investment* you won't regret. When you have questions about recipes, baking terminology, how to measure, equivalent measures, substitutions, baking tools and how to use them, melting chocolates, microwave hints, exploring new items for your product line, how to garnish a dessert, or how to decorate cakes (both simple and elaborate), 99 percent of the time reliable information and answers will be as close as your bookshelf. Collecting can be fun. Enjoy!

1. Quality ingredients are necessary for quality products. Using inferior ingredients will most certainly result in mediocre products. While cost is a major consideration in operating your business, don't automatically go after the cheapest ingredients you can find. Less expensive brands or substitutes often don't give the desired results. The more specific or finely tuned your ingredients, the better your products. In my opinion, there is no match for pure butter. If the recipe gives a choice of butter or margarine, use butter. People that know quality can immediately taste the difference. There is also a distinct difference in the taste of products made with pure vanilla extract and imitation vanilla. Pure vanilla is more expensive but well worth the

cost. Also, be careful to choose the right type of flour for the product you're making. Flour is processed differently for use in different products. Most recipes are specific about the type of flour that works best in the product.

2. Always use the right mixer attachment. If you've never used a mixer that has different beaters, take the time to *read the manual* that came with the mixer. Identify the attachment that works best for the task you're performing. Three attachments (wire whip, dough hook, and paddle) are usually included with the purchase of a stand mixer such as a KitchenAid or commercial mixer. If you purchased a used mixer and didn't receive a manual, the following general information will be helpful. The flat beater or paddle is usually best for normal-to-heavy mixtures, such as cakes, cheesecakes, creamed frosting, candies, cookies, pie pastry, and quick breads. The wire whip is usually best for mixtures that need air incorporated, such as eggs, egg whites, heavy cream, boiled frostings, sponge cakes, angel food cakes, and some candies. The dough hook is best for mixing and kneading yeast dough for breads, rolls, coffee cakes, and buns. To achieve the best results, use the proper tools.

3. Make your life a little easier. When baking cookies, use parchment paper on the cookie sheets before dropping on the cookie dough. Using parchment paper will result in less pan washing. When you have a large quantity of cookies to bake, fewer pans to wash means less labor.

4. Measuring. Your customers want and expect consistency. They're expecting the same taste, size, texture, and appearance that they purchased previously. Properly measuring ingredients is very important to the consistency of your products. Here are a few tips that will help. Use liquid measuring cups to measure liquids, dry measuring cups to measure dry or solid ingredients, and standard measuring spoons to measure small amounts of dry or liquid ingredients. When measuring a liquid, don't hold the cup in your hand. Place the cup on a flat surface, pour in the liquid, then read it at eye level. To measure dry ingredients (like granulated sugar or flour) use the measuring cup that holds the exact amount called for in the recipe, spoon it lightly into the cup, then level it off with the straight edge of a knife or spatula. Do not shake to level. The same method should be used with

measuring spoons. Brown sugar should be packed firmly in the cup before leveling. When measuring solids like peanut butter or vegetable shortening, first spray the inside of the dry measuring cup with vegetable cooking spray (this makes release from the cup easier), then pack the cup firmly before leveling.

5. Liquid consistency. Maybe you've never thought that eggs are a part of the liquid in your products. Maybe you've noticed that the standards for egg sizes seem to vary a little from supplier to supplier and time to time. This can create a problem with the amount of liquid in each batch of product that you mix. Variations in the size of eggs is definitely a problem when making cookies. The slightest bit more liquid will cause the dough to be softer and the cookies to spread more when baking. Now you have a larger but thinner cookie. This is the inconsistency that your customers will not appreciate. If this becomes a concern or problem for you, try measuring the eggs in a liquid measuring cup or weighing them. Use the same measure or weight of eggs each time to keep your liquid content consistent.

6. Get to know your oven. The internal temperature in one oven could be different from another oven even when the same settings are used. Test your oven. When necessary, adjust the temperature settings called for in the recipe.

7. Creating your own recipe book. Don't rely on memory for all of your recipes, particularly the ones that you create. Mistaken recall of just one ingredient can change the product in taste if not in appearance. If this happens, you probably won't be aware of it, but your customers will taste the difference. Don't write your recipes on scraps of paper or miscellaneous scratch pads. Buy a notebook. Dedicate it to recipes only, and keep it in a safe place. Your recipes are prized possessions. Treat them that way.

CHAPTER 17

WHERE TO FIND IT

BAKING EQUIPMENT AND TOOLS

Used Commercial Baking Equipment: Ovens, Mixers, Sinks, Tables, and More

These can be found through your local newspaper and the yellow pages. Check under "Restaurant Equipment," "Business Equipment," or "Bakery Equipment." Also search the Internet using the categories just mentioned. Don't forget to put your city and state in the online search box along with the category. In addition to searching for the best equipment at the best price, your aim is to purchase any large or heavy equipment as close to your work place as possible. The shorter the delivery distance, the less you pay for delivery. Always be mindful of your budget.

New Commercial Baking Equipment: Ovens, Mixers, Sinks, Tables, Utensils, and More

Direct South ~ 866-543-4349 ~ www.directsouth.com
Hubert ~ 800-543-7374 ~ www.hubert.com
Restaurant Depot ~ 718-939-6400 ~ www.restaurantdepot.com
Superior Products ~ 800-328-9800 ~ www.superprod.com

KitchenAid Mixers and Food Processors

Costco Wholesale ~ Customer Service: 800-727-8248 ~ www.costco.com
KitchenAid Company ~ Customer Service: 800-541-
     6390 ~ www.kitchenaid.com
QVC ~ 800-345-1515 ~ www.qvc.com
Sam's Club ~ Customer Service: 888-746-7726 ~ www.samsclub.com
Wal-Mart, Target, home specialty stores (Home
     Depot, Lowe's), and department stores

Baking Pans, Cake Decorating Supplies, and More

Cake Art ~ 404-294-5005 (local shopping only
     in the metro Atlanta, GA area)
Direct South, Inc. ~ 866-543-4349 ~ www.directsouth.com
Everything Special ~ 770-961-0750 (local shopping
     in the metro Atlanta, GA area)
Hubert ~ 800-543-7374 ~ www.hubert.com
Michaels ~ 800-642-4235 ~ www.michaels.com
Parrish's Supplies ~ 800-736-8443 ~ www.parrishsmagicline.com
Party City ~ www.partycity.com
Superior Products ~ 800-328-9800 ~ www.superprod.com
Wilton ~ 800-794-5866 ~ www.wilton.com
Local stores ~ Check your yellow pages under "Baking Supplies,"
     "Cake Decorating" or "Hobby and Crafts."

WHOLESALE FOOD SUPPLIES
(Specializing in baking ingredients)

Costco Wholesale ~ 800-727-8248 ~ www.costco.com
Sam's Club ~ 888-746-7726 ~ www.samsclub.com
Sutherland's Foodservice ~ 404-366-8550 (serving
     only the metro Atlanta, GA area)
Tropical Nut & Fruit ~ 800-544-3762 ~ www.tropicalfoods.com

Restaurant Depot ~ 718-939-6400 ~ www.restaurantdepot.com

Local companies ~ Check the yellow pages for additional
   wholesale and discount food suppliers in your area.

Always compare quality, quantity, and prices before you buy.

WHOLESALE GOURMET FOODS

The following companies specialize in prepackaged and bulk gourmet foods: popcorn (in many flavors), cookies, chips, crackers, pretzels, candy (in any flavor and assortment you can imagine), cheese straws, mustards, sauces, nuts (raw, roasted, candied, and more), snack mixes (incredible assortments), cakes, pies, coffee, tea, cocoa, cappuccino, and more!

Buddy Squirrel ~ 800-972-2658 ~ www.qcbs.com

Chicago Coffee Roastery ~ 800-762-5402 ~ www.chicagocoffee.com

Cloverland Sweets ~ 800-523-3505

The Crickle Company ~ 800-237-8689 ~ www.cricklecompany.com

Crown Mulling Spices ~ 800-738-9227 ~ www.crownspices.com

Dillon Candy Company ~ 800-382-8338 ~ www.dilloncandy.com

D'Marie ~ 877-778-0707 ~ www.dmarieinc.com

Eagle's Peak Gourmet ~ 800-421-4951 ~ www.eaglespeakgourmet.com

East Shore Specialty Foods ~ 800-236-1069 ~ www.eastshorefoods.com

Gift Basket Supplies ~ 800-428-0522 ~ www.giftbasketsupplies.com

Gourmet Center ~ 800-422-2924 ~ www.biscoff.com

Graffiti Zoo ~ 866-294-3555 ~ www.graffitizoo.com

J&M Foods ~ 800-264-2278 ~ www.jm-foods.com

Judi's Confections and Gourmet Gifts ~
   770-754-1481 ~ www.judisconfections.com

Kennedy Gourmet ~ 866-986-3227 ~ www.kennedygourmet.com

Mississippi Cheese Straw Factory ~ 800-530-
   7496 ~ www.mscheesestraws.com

Nancy's Candy Co. ~ 800-328-3834 ~ www.nancysfudge.com

Neighbors Coffee ~ 800-299-9016 ~ www.neighborscoffee.com

Noble Popcorn Farms ~ 800-537-9554 ~ www.noblepopcorn.com

Peters Imports ~ 800-541-8267 ~ www.petersimports.com

Plentiful Pantry ~ 800-727-8284 ~ www.plentifulpantry.com

Queen City Coffee Company ~ 800-487-7460 ~ www.queencitycoffee.com

Robicheaux's Specialty Candy ~ 800-688-1941 ~

www.shop.store.yahoo.com\robicheauxcandy

Rowena's ~ 800-627-8699 ~ www.rowenas.com

Saralyn's Shortbread ~ 877-727-2596 ~ www.saralynshortbread.com

Sisters Gourmet ~ 877-338-1388 ~ www.sistersgourmet.com

Tracy-Luckey Co. ~ 800-476-4796 ~ www.tracy-luckey.com

Tropical ~ 800-544-3762 ~ www.tropicalfoods.com

Yam Good Pies ~ 706-882-3456 ~ www.oulalasweets.com

Young Pecan Plantations ~ 800-440-6442 ~ www.

youngpecanplantations.com

Request samples if you're not familiar with a product, want to see the exact size or color, or need to sample it before promoting it to your customers. Many companies will send a free sample. Some charge for samples plus shipping and handling. When you call to request samples, introduce yourself with a company name. That will increase your chances of receiving *free* samples.

GOURMET GIFT SETS

This company takes the hassle, frustration, and a lot of labor out of making gift baskets. It offers theme, premade gourmet gift sets. These baskets are filled with quality food components, shrink-wrapped (to ensure arrival in good condition), and delivered to you ready to sell.

BoxCo Industries ~ 800-654-2932 ~ www.boxcoindustries.com

GIFT PACKAGING SOURCES

Here you can find gift boxes, tissue paper, ribbon, gift tote bags, gift basket supplies, baskets, tins, custom gift boxes, custom labels, specialty candy and nut bags, custom ribbons, and more.

Allsorts Premium Packaging ~ 888-565-9727 ~ www.allsortswrap.com

Bags & Bows ~ 800-225-8155 ~ www.bagsandbowsonline.com

Bertels Can Company ~ 800-829-0578 ~ www.bertelscan.com

BoxCo Industries~ 800-654-2932 ~ www.boxcoindustries.com

Burton & Burton ~ 800-241-2094 ~ www.burtonandburton.com

Can Creations ~ 800-272-0235 ~ www.cancreations.com

Carolina Retail Packaging ~ 800-868-5878 ~ www.carolinaretail.com

Collector's Gallery ~ 800-346-3063 ~ www.collectorsgallery.org

Del Rey Graphics ~ 800-533-5739 ~ www.delreygraphics.com

Gift Box Corporation ~ 800-443-8269 ~ www.800giftbox.com

Matthews Hamper House ~ 404-366-7166 ~ www.
       matthewshamperhouse.com

Nashville Wraps ~ 800-547-9727 ~ www.nashvillewraps.com

The Packaging Source ~ 800-624-6244 ~ www.packagingsource.com

Premier Packaging ~ 800-203-5558 ~ www.retailpackaging.com

Presentation Packaging ~ 800-818-2698 ~ www.
       presentationpackaging.com

Roof Basket Works ~ 800-368-8425 ~ www.roofbasket.com

SampleHouse ~ 800-626-2645 ~ www.samplehouse.com

Spectrum Ascona ~ 800-356-1473 ~ www.asconapkg.com

Summerfield Packaging ~ 800-826-8427 ~ www.summerfieldpkg.com

U.S. Box Corp. ~ 800-221-0999 ~ www.usbox.com

Willow Specialties ~ 800-724-7300 ~ www.willowspecialties.com

Request samples if you're not familiar with a product, want to see the exact size or color, or need to sample it before promoting it to your customers. Many companies will send a free sample. Some companies charge for samples plus shipping and handling. When you call to request samples, introduce yourself with a company name. That will increase your chances of receiving *free* samples.

BALLOONS

If you're interested in starting a balloon business or want to add balloons to your existing product line, Burton & Burton has balloons for almost every occasion. They carry sizes from small to extra large. They also carry items that complement the balloons, such as mugs, tote bags, stuffed animals, vases, and decorative ceramic pieces.

Burton & Burton ~ 800-241-2094 ~ www.burtonandburton.com

SPECIALTY PAPERS

These companies can assist you with giving your business a professional and polished look. They carry almost everything that you might need in terms of fancy stationery, brochure paper, border design paper for flyers, theme postcards, theme business cards, newsletter paper, note cards, and envelopes. They also carry presentation stands and equipment.

Idea Art ~ 800-433-2278 ~ www.ideaart.com
Kinko's, Office Depot, OfficeMax, and Staples
Masterpiece Studios ~ 800-447-0219 ~ www.masterpiecestudios.com
PaperDirect ~ 800-272-7377 ~ www.paperdirect.com

YOUR PRODUCT IN PICTURES

Have you ever seen business cards or postcards with an eye-catching photo of the company's product? The following companies can provide similar presentation pieces for you. They also offer full-color brochures and catalogs.

Image Graphics ~ 866-334-5432 ~ www.imagegraphics.com
Kinko's ~ www.fedexkinkos.com or visit your local store
Office Depot ~ 800-463-3768 ~ www.officedepot.com
PulseDirect ~ 800-411-6256 ~ www.postcardpower.com

PUT YOUR STAMP ON IT

Labels can be an important of your advertising. In addition to product information, labels tell the receiver of your products or creations where and how you can be reached. Labels also give the package a professional look. The following companies offer a large variety of label sizes and colors in both stock and custom designs.

Bags & Bows ~ 800-225-8155 ~ www.bagsandbowsonline.com
Century Marketing ~ 800-537-9429 ~ www.centurylabel.com
Gift Box Corporation ~ 800-443-8269 ~ www.800giftbox.com
Interstate Label Company ~ 800-426-3261 ~ www.interstatelabel.com
Nashville Wraps ~ 800-547-9727 ~ www.nashvillewraps.com
Summerfield Packaging ~ 800-826-8427 ~ www.summerfieldpkg.com

GIFT PACKAGING EQUIPMENT

If you're making gift baskets, you'll need a heat gun for shrink wrapping. If you're packaging cookies, nuts, or candy, you will need a heat sealer or crimping iron. If you don't have the time or the ability to make handmade bows, a bow machine can help you with that task. The following companies carry a selection of equipment and supplies that will assist you in creating the perfect package or gift.

AllSorts Premium Packaging ~ 888-565-9727 ~ www.allsortswrap.com
Bags & Bows ~ 800-225-8155 ~ www.bagsandbowsonline.com
Burton & Burton ~ 800-241-2094 ~ www.burtonandburton.com
Can Creations ~ 800-272-0235 ~ www.cancreations.com
Nashville Wraps ~ 800-547-9727 ~ www.nashvillewraps.com

PACKING AND SHIPPING SUPPLIES

The thought of missing out on a sale or a contract simply because you cannot pack and ship your products at an affordable rate is very disheartening. In order to compete in the shipping category, you must be able to buy supplies at wholesale prices. The following companies carry a full line of packing and shipping supplies.

Chiswick ~ 800-225-8708 ~ www.chiswick.com
ULINE ~ 800-295-5510 ~ www.uline.com
Local grocery store ~ Good source for dry ice in small quantities.
Local shipping supply companies ~ Check your yellow pages or online.

BAKERY PACKAGING AND SUPPLIES

Fulton Paper Co. ~ 800-282-2551 ~ www.fultonpaper.com
Hubert ~ 800-543-7374 ~ www.hubert.com
Instawares ~ 800-892-3622 ~ www.instawares.com
Market Grocery ~ 404-361-8620 (serving only the metro Atlanta, GA area)
Restaurant Depot ~ 718-939-6400 ~ www.restaurantdepot.com
Sutherlands Foodservice ~ 404-366-8550 (serving
        only the metro Atlanta, GA area)

PROMOTIONAL AND ADVERTISING ITEMS

In addition to the companies listed below, there are hundreds of companies that offer promotional items. They can be found online (the Internet) or the yellow pages.

Best Impressions ~ 800-635-2378 ~ www.bestimpressions.com
4imprint ~ 877-446-7746 ~ www.4imprint.com
Kinko's ~ www.fedexkinkos.com or visit your local store

FOOD INDUSTRY MAGAZINES

These publications will keep you updated on the latest food and market trends, both retail and wholesale.

Fancy Food & Culinary Products ~ www.fancyfoodmagazine.com
Gourmet News ~ www.gourmetnews.com

When you shopping for packaging supplies, locate as many sources as possible that carry the items you need. Compare for best prices, and then look for the company nearest you. The closer the company, the bigger your savings on shipping.

SERVICE WITH A SMILE

Good customer service can strengthen your business, promote it, and help it to flourish. It can be one of the biggest reasons that people continue to do business with you. On the other hand, poor customer service can easily drive people away and cause your business to suffer. When you establish rules or create policies, always think of how you can endear your business to your customers and keep them happy. When your customer has a complaint about your products or service, ask yourself if the situation were reversed, how would you like to be treated. *Many people believe that it's easier to keep a customer than to get a new one.*

ABOUT THE AUTHOR

My love and fascination for baking started when my grandmother Hattie would let me help her with making cakes, cookies, pies, and a family favorite, bread pudding. In the beginning, I was too small and too young to operate the stove, so she let me do the safe things like breaking eggs and measuring ingredients. It wasn't long before I graduated to using the stove and being in the kitchen without supervision. Throughout the years, baking and collecting recipes continued to be my favorite hobbies. At holiday time, I always had more requests for baked goods than I could handle.

In 1985, I resigned my position with a railway company in Atlanta, Georgia. While I pondered my next employment move, a dear friend, Thelma Ann, urged me to start a baking business. I was very reluctant and not sure that I could bake well enough to earn a living. My friend insisted that I could, and a year or so later, I proved her right. I started a home-based baking business that featured a variety of frosted cakes, cheesecakes, and pound cakes.

Throughout the years, my curiosity and sometimes dissatisfaction led me to try many different things within the food and gift industry. My twenty-plus years in the business have been spent providing specialty desserts and gourmet gifts to restaurants, dessert cafés, delicatessens, hotels, private clubs, colleges, hospitals, commercial real-estate management companies, TV news anchors, and some of the most prestigious corporations at the Atlanta Financial Center.

Owning and operating a home-based baking business has been profitable, fun, exciting, challenging, frustrating, and a tremendous learning experience! All of these experiences have compelled me to write this book, which I hope is the beginning of the next chapter of my career.

Quincella C. Geiger